Christianity, Slavery & Labour

by CHAPMAN COHEN

One Shilling and Sixpence

Christianity Slavery & Labour

Published by:
Research Associates School Times Publications
&
Frontline Distribution International Inc.
Chicago. Jamaica. London. Republic of Trinidad and Tobago.
5206 S. Harper Avenue, Chicgo, Illinois, 60615

Christianity Slavery & Labour

Published 2010
Research Associates School Times Publications
Frontline Distribution Int'L Inc.
Published in the Caribbean by: Miguel Lorne Publishers & Frontline

First Published in 1931

ISBN: 0-948390-91-3

CONTENTS

I.

Slavery and the Bible

▼ ▼

It has become an article of faith with the modern Christian that by some means, unspecified, and at some time, unknown, Christianity abolished the slave trade. Bearing in mind the fact that it was not until the middle of the nineteenth century that slavery became illegal in Christian countries, with the exception of Abyssinia, where it still exists, and that even then Christian slave-owners had to be bought out in some cases and *fought* out in others; remembering, also, that the traffic in human flesh flourished right through those centuries when Christianity was most powerful, the claim seems difficult of understanding. It is still harder to justify it by an appeal to facts. But the force of repetition is great; it is, in fact, taken by vast masses of people as the equivalent of proof. To repeat certain statements, while ignoring all rebutting facts, is a sure way of carrying conviction to the minds of thousands. And thus it happens that the particular claim we have mentioned is accepted as a statement of mere historic truth by the vast majority of modern believers.

A typical statement of the case is made by Canon W. R. Brownlow, in his "Slavery and Serfdom in Europe." On the very first page of that volume he presents his readers with the following :—

> At a time when people are asking what benefits the Christian religion conferred upon the human race, the abolition of slavery is at once a ready and a valid answer.

We are not told when or where Christianity did this; and the Canon's pages bear evidence that slavery flourished under Christian auspices without Christians seeing anything radically wrong in its existence. All he shows is that some Christians did a little towards making the lot of the slave tolerable, and that some Christians favoured emancipation. One would expect nothing less. It is to the credit of human nature that no creed, political or religious, is ever able to altogether suppress its finer impulses. But it is the influence of Christians as such, and of the Christian Churches as a whole, with which one is really concerned.

Anyhow, it is this claim that we shall examine in the following pages. It will not be necessary to discuss the question of the origin or nature of slavery, nor of its connection with particular phases of economic life. Our purpose is a simpler and a more restricted one. It is to examine the relation—historical and doctrinal—which has existed between Christianity and the slave trade. And an impartial examination of the facts will show, not alone that slavery is countenanced by the Christian Scriptures, but that as an institution it flourished under Christian rule, was never formally prohibited by the Christian church, was revived under Christian auspices when various social causes threatened its disappearance, and in modern times added a measure of degradation to the lot of the slave that was unknown to antiquity.

That a direct sanction for slavery is given in the Old Testament admits of no question. The twenty-fifth chapter of Leviticus gives explicit instruction of whom slaves are to be bought, with the proviso that a Hebrew slave may be redeemed. The "Children of the strangers" are to be an inheritance "for your children forever.' In the year of Jubilee the Hebrew slave could claim his freedom, but "if his master have given him a wife," and there are children, "the wife and her children shall be her masters, and he shall go out by himself."[1] This separation of the family formed one of the most repulsive features of American slavery, but it is enough to note here the Scriptural warranty for the practice. If, however, the claims of family prove stronger than the love of freedom and the slave declines to leave wife and children, then the master shall bring the slave to the doorpost of the house, bore his ear through with an awl, and he must remain his

[1] Exodus xxi. 25.

slave forever. If a master struck his slave and killed him on the spot he was to be "surely punished," but if the slave lingered for a day or two the master went unpunished, for the slave was "his money." On this point the Bible compares but ill with the Koran:

> God hath ordained that your brothers should be your slaves; therefore let him whom God hath ordained to be the slave of his brother, his brother must give him of the clothes wherewith he clotheth himself, and not order him to do anything beyond his power. . . . A man who illtreats his slave will not enter paradise.

So, also, as against the Biblical rule above noted, we may place Mohammed's injunction: "Whoever is the cause of separation between mother and child by selling and giving, God will separate him from his friends on the day of resurrection."

There is only one other point that deserves noting, and that is the *price* of human beings as fixed by the God of the Bible. The price was not fixed for the purpose of purchasing slaves, but it may stand. It will be found in the 27th chapter of Leviticus, and if we calculate the value of the silver shekel as about two shillings and sixpence, the price works out as follows: From one month to five years, a male 12s. 6d., female, 7s. 6d.; from five to twenty, male, £3 15s., female, 25s.; from twenty to sixty, male, £6 5s., female, £3 15s. We have never heard of any Christian in a court of law using this divine valuation in order to claim compensation, but in a genuinely Christian community it might be done.

In the New Testament there is no abrogation of the slave laws of the Bible. Archdeacon Paley, special pleader as he is, is forced to admit that there " is no passage in the Christian Scriptures by which it (slavery) is condemned or prohibited."[2] Still, he claims that " by the mild diffusion of its light and influence " Christianity tends to overcome wrong. But a light must be very feeble, and its influence poor, if it takes hundreds of years to make itself felt, particularly when we find it revived and re-established under Christian rule, and when it had almost disappeared from the Western world. To the same end Pope Leo III. remarks in his letter of 1888 to the Bishops of Brazil :—

> When amid the slave multitude whom she has numbered among her children, some led astray by some hope of liberty, have had recourse to violence and sedition, the Church has always condemned these unlawful efforts, and through her ministers has applied the remedy of patience. . . . St. Peter was addressing himself specially to slaves when he wrote : " For this is thankworthy, if for conscience towards God a man endure sorrows, suffering wrongfully."

How a preaching of patience under admitted wrong could help to destroy slavery it is puzzling to discover.

[2] *Moral Philosophy*. Sec. " Slavery."

So far as Jesus is concerned, he nowhere sets his face against slavery. He accepted slavery as he accepted all the other institutions and superstitions around him. Nothing was further from his mind than a social revolution, or even social reform. Slaves or serfs in revolt never looked to Jesus for inspiration, but slave-owner and feudal lord have invariably held him up as an ideal for those under them. And in addition to giving a teaching of non-resistance and passive obedience fatal to real freedom and independence, we have in Luke xvii. 7-10 a peculiarly revolting exposition of the relation of master and slave. Later, we shall see how the figure of the Gospel Jesus and the teachings of the New Testament were used in modern times to ward off attacks by Abolitionists on the institution of slavery.

I have used the word " slave " instead of the New Testament " servant " because " servant " has no right there at all. The Greek word which in the N.T. is translated " servant," is so translated nowhere else. Everywhere but here it is translated " slave." Yet, in the more than one hundred places in which the word occurs, we get uniformly " servant." The reason for this is obvious; to have rendered it " slave " would have come as a shock to simple-minded believers, since it would have placed the N.T. clearly on the side of the slave-owner. Honesty of interpretation was thus sacrificed to convenience, and the New

Testament endorsement of slavery is concealed from the unwary.

Paul's teaching on the question of slavery is clear and explicit. His general advice is that people are to abide in that condition in which they are at the time of conversion, whether it be married or single, bond or free. Servants (*i.e.,* slaves) are to be obedient to their masters in fear and trembling, giving them the same absolute submission as they give to Christ; they are to submit themselves to every ordinance of man; to be subject, not only to the good, but also to the bad, "with all fear," for God is pleased when his servants bear wrong patiently. And, adding practice to precept, the runaway slave Onesimus is sent back to his master, albeit with the admonition that he is to be treated with kindness.[3] In the face of both text and practice, it is difficult to find any justification for the plea that slavery owes its abolition to the influence or teaching of Christianity.

It is not surprising to find the Rev. L. O. Agate admits that "There is no explicit condemnation in the teaching of our Lord. . . . It remains true that the abolitionist could point to no one text in the Gospels in defence of his position, while those who defended slavery could appeal at any rate to the letter of Scripture.[4]

[3] See Eph. c. 6; First Peter ii.; 1 Cor. vii.; Ep. to Philemon.

[4] *Encyclopedia of Religion and Ethics.* Vol II. p. 602.

So far Biblical Christianity. Slavery was, indeed, not peculiar to Christian or Biblical teaching. It was common to the whole of the ancient world, and there is neither intention nor necessity to minimise its evils. Our question now is, however, as to the influence exerted by Christianity on the institution, and to answer that question it is necessary to deal with slavery as it existed in the old Roman Empire, and particularly with the state of law and opinion at the time when Christianity began to exert a commanding influence in the State.

II.

Paganism and Slavery

▼ ▼

"WHOEVER," says Pope Leo XIII., "compares the Pagan and the Christian attitude towards slavery will easily come to the conclusion that the one was marked by great cruelty and wickedness, and the other by great gentleness and humanity."[5] It is, of course, vain for anyone to assert that ancient slavery did not involve cruelty and injustice; all slavery does. That is part of the case against the system. But anyone who compares ancient slavery with modern negro slavery—a system that was actually instituted by Christians—will find it hard to point out in what direction the modern was an improvement on the ancient slavery, while it is easy to show that in some respects it was distinctly worse. And there is always the important distinction that, while ancient slavery represented a phase of social development, and tended to something better, modern, or Christian, slavery stood for a deliberate retrogression in social life.

It is not to our purpose to deal with the beginnings

[5] Letter to the Bishops of Brazil; 1888.

of slavery in the Roman State. It was common to the whole of the ancient world, and had its origin in the same set of circumstances. That the master possessed in the earlier stages unlimited power over his slaves is also clear, as is also the inevitable consequence that brutal treatment existed. But there were several circumstances that tended to improve the lot of the slave in Rome There was, first of all, the fact that Roman slavery had grown out ot the social life of the period. Men became slaves through defeat in war, or as a punishment, their slavery thus representing a stroke of ill-fortune. And there was no distinction of colour. The Roman or the Greek, might consider himself superior to others, but his superiority was based on considerations that were personal, national, or cultural. When Rome conquered a people, absorption in the empire almost automatically brought a share in the empire's dignities and privileges. Inter-marriage took place, and, as Lord Cromer says :—

> The dominant Roman and the intellectual Greek thought themselves, without doubt very superior to the savage Gaul or Briton, and to the more civilized Egyptian or Asiatic, but in estimating his sense of superiority neither appears, so far as I can judge, to have taken much account of whether the skin of the subject or less intellectually advanced races were white, black, or brown.[6]

The theory that the control of the world should rest

[6] *Ancient and Modern Imperialism*, p. 140.

with the white races is a modern theory, and, as a consequence, colour has in modern times carried with it a badge of inferiority, of divinely ordained servitude. Roman religion was polytheistic, inclusive, and tolerant. Christianity was monotheistic, exclusive, and intolerant. And as the latter extended its sway over the world of politics it introduced the spirit of exclusiveness and intolerance into all departments of life. "Saved" and "lost" in theology were the equivalents of superior and inferior in sociology. And as the overwhelming bulk of the coloured people remained outside the Christian pale, the development of the colour bar was easy. Christianity gave just that religious sanction which slavery required for its ethical justification. Slavery applied to whites was revolting; slavery applied to blacks became part of the divinely appointed order.

Next, because slavery was, so to speak, native in ancient society, the growth of ethical sentiment and of legislation tended to eliminate the harsher features of the system, and to move in the direction of its abolition. From the ethical side it admits of no question that there existed in the days of the Empire a body of teaching that in principle struck at the whole institution of slavery. Plato and Aristotle, Zeno and Epicurus, in Athens, had dwelt upon the duty of kindness to slaves, as also Seneca, and many other writers in Rome. It was Zeno, the founder of Stoicism, who declared that "all men are by nature equal, virtue alone creates differences between them," a sentiment that would have shocked the slave-owning Christian of the nineteenth century. It was Seneca who said: "Live gently and kindly with your slave, and admit him to conversation with you, to council with you, and to a share in your meals." And, again: "No one is precluded from virtue; it lies open to all, welcome to all, invites all, whether well-born, freedmen, slaves, kings, or exiles. . . . Men's bodies may be subject to masters, but the mind remains independent." "Remember," he says, "that he whom you call your slave sprang from the same stock, is smiled upon by the same skies, and on equal terms with yourself breathes, lives, and dies." "As an Antonine," said Marcus Aurelius, "I belong to Rome, as a man to the world." "Slavery," according to the universal opinion of Roman lawyers, "is an institution of the law of nations, by which one man is made the property of another contrary to natural right." They explained that "Wars arose and in their train followed captivity and then slavery, which is contrary to the law of nature; for by that law all men are born originally free.'"[7] It was the Christian who elaborated the theory that black slavery was permissible because the whole of the dark-skinned people were suffering from the curse God pronounced on Ham, the son of Noah.

[7] See Sandar's *Institutes of Justinian,* pp. 8-15.

There is no need to multiply quotations concerning a question on which information is so easily available. It is enough that the Romans did not attempt to justify slavery on the ground of either morality or religion. That was left for the Christian Church. It was contrary to natural law, as the Romans distinguished between that and civil law, and it brought no necessary individual nor personal inferiority. It was purely a "law of nations," and however desirable it might be, it had no other foundation than the power of one class to enslave another.

Finally, it is important that one's judgment should not be confused by identifying ancient slavery with that form of slavery which originated under Christian auspices. We are apt to think of the ancient slave as being identical with the miserable and degraded being that disgraced Christian countries less than a century ago. This, however, is far from the truth. The Roman slave did not, of necessity, lack education. Slaves were to be found who were doctors, writers, poets, philosophers, and moralists. Plautus, Phaedrus, Terence, Epictetus, were slaves. Slaves were the intimates of men of all stations of life, even of the emperor. Certainly it never dawned on the Roman mind to prohibit education to the slave. That was left for the Christian world, and almost within our own time. Thus in South Carolina, as late as 1834, it was enacted that any person who taught a slave to read or write should be fined one hundred dollars and be imprisoned not more than six months. In Virginia, in 1849, the punishment for this offence was the same. In Georgia the fine was the same, with punishment at "the discretion of the Court." In Louisiana it was twelve months' imprisonment, and in Alabama a fine of from 200 to 500 dollars.[8]

Mr. R. H. Barrow, in a recent and important work, says:—

Neither the crushing of individuality nor the refusal of personal growth was necessarily inherent in Roman slavery . . . In outward appearance he (the slave) did not differ from the free man; neither colour nor clothing revealed his condition; he witnessed the same games as the freeman; he shared in the life of the municipal towns, even contributing what he was allowed, and sometimes at least sharing equally in bequests made to it. . . . Between the slave and the free there often seems to have been little social barrier. . . . We have seen slaves and freedmen working together in the factory and office, sitting as fellow members of the same college and sharing the expenses of offering or tomb.[9]

[8] Cairnes. *The Slave Power,* pp. 105-6.

[9] Slavery *in the Roman Empire.* 1928. pp. 52-170. See also an equally important work, *Freedmen in the Early Roman Empire.* 1929. p. 99.

Professor Cairnes very aptly draws the distinction between Pagan and Christian slavery :—

> In antiquity precautions were taken to prevent the slave from breaking his chains; at the present day measures are adopted to deprive him even of the desire of freedom. The ancients kept the bodies of their slaves in bondage, but they placed no restraint upon the mind and no check upon education; and they acted consistently with their principle, since a natural termination of slavery existed, and one day or other the slave might be set free, and become the equal of his master. . . . The education of slaves amongst the ancients prepared the way for emancipation. The prohibition of the education of slaves amongst the moderns has naturally suggested the policy of holding them in perpetual bondage.[10]

In a larger degree the slave in Rome, in addition to his employment in agriculture and in the household, engaged in all trades and trading. The whole field of trade and industry was open to the slave, and Professor Dill comes close to the facts when he says that "The slave class of antiquity really corresponded to our free labouring class."[11] In addition we have to note that a well-conducted slave, by his own earnings, was able to purchase his freedom in the course of a few years. The result of this, along with the very frequent manumissions, either during the lifetime of a master or at his death, motived not, as Professor Dill

[10] *The Slave Power,* pp. 106-7.

[11] *Roman Society From Nero to Marcus Aurelius,* p. 102.

remarks, by religious feeling, but "by the natural human wish to make some return to faithful servants or to leave a memory of kindness behind," was to create a movement between the slave class proper and the Roman citizen not greatly unlike that by which the lower middle class in English society gradually merges in a higher social stratum.

It will not do, therefore, to identify Pagan with Christian slavery. Slavery as an institution existed in both cases, but, as Professor Cairnes says, "we look in vain in the records of antiquity for a traffic which in extent, in systematic character . . . can be regarded as the analogue of the modern slave trade." The Christian slave trade represents one of the most frightful and systematic brutalities the world has ever known.

Finally, it remains to indicate the tendency of Roman law in relation to slavery. In the earlier stage of Roman history the master possessed absolute power over the slave, although its exercise was conditioned by the considerations set forth above. But for several centuries antedating the rise of Christianity to power there had been a progressive movement in the direction of giving the slave a definite legal status. The consequence was a series of enactments curtailing considerably the power of the master over the slave.

Masters were prohibited sending their slaves into the arena without a judicial sentence. Claudius punished, as a murderer, any master who killed his slave. Nero appointed judges to hear the complaints of slaves as to ill-treatment or insufficient feeding. Domitian forbade the mutilation of slaves; Hadrian forbade the selling of slaves to gladiators, destroyed private prisons for them, and ordered that they who were proved to have ill-treated their slaves should be forced to sell them. Diocletian forbade a free man to sell himself into slavery. Man-stealers were punished with death. In the interpretation of wills it was also to be assumed that the slave family was not to be separated.[12] Caracalla forbade the selling of children into slavery, and in other directions all encouragement was given to acts of manumission.[13] No wonder Lecky says :—

> When we add to these laws the broad maxims of equity asserting the essential equality of the human race which the jurists had borrowed from the Stoics, and which supplied the principles to guide the judges in their decisions, it must be admitted that the slave code of Imperial Rome compares not unfavourably with those of some Christian nations.[14]

To the question whether Christianity had anything

[12] The humanity of this last provision stands out in striking contrast to the practice in Christian countries in the nineteenth century.

[13] It became a dictum of the Roman Law that all doubtful cases involving slavery should be decided in favour of liberty. See Lea, *Studies in Church History,* pp. 536-7.

[14] *Hist. of European Morals,* I., p. 308.

to do with this growth of humanitarian, Mr. A. M. Duff answers emphatically, No. He says: In legislation it had no influence; to the most enlightened government of the second century Christians were still a traitorous and an obstinate sect that clung to a ridiculous Eastern superstition. Nor can any influence on imperial policy be traced through Stoicism to a Christian source.[15]

All that need be added to this is that the later Christian slavery represented a distinct retrogression, deliberately revived from motives of sheer cupidity, and accompanied by more revolting features than the slavery of ancient times.

Had Christianity been really and inevitably averse to slavery, it had, as we have seen, a movement of both opinion and law on which to base its liberalizing efforts. What are the facts?

It has already been pointed out that in the New Testament nothing is to be found in the shape of a condemnation of the institution of slavery. In this respect it stands far below the best ethical teaching of antiquity. In addition, we have in the Christian writings a teaching of obedience that impressed the slave with the pious obligation of remaining content in his servitude, and of rendering all honour and obedience to his owner. From its first rise to power, this was characteristic of Christian teaching. On the better

[15] *Freedmen in the Early Roman Empire*, p. 196.

aspects of the civic and political life of the ancient world Christianity fell as a blight. Slaves were being rapidly transferred into freemen—so rapidly that their growth alarmed the more conservative element in Roman society.[16] Christianity met the movement by turning freemen into slaves. Under Paganism, bodies only were enslaved; minds were left free. Christianity enslaved both body and mind. The nature of this process is well indicated by Professor Seeley :—

> Liberty is force of character roused by the sense of wrong. . . . Such was not the Christian spirit. In this when it was genuine there was no rebellion, there was no assertion of right. Those who practised it were not less obedient, but more obedient than others; they had no turn for liberty; they had no quarrel with the despotism of the Cæsars. . . . Christianity confirmed as much as it controlled despotism. It produced a complete change in the attitude of the people to the Emperor. . . . It strengthened in them the feeling of submissive reverence for government as such, it encouraged the dispositions of the time to political passiveness. It was intensely conservative, and gave to power with one hand as much as it took away with the other. Constantine, if he was influenced by policy was influenced by a wise policy, when he extended his patronage to the Church. By so doing he may be said to have purchased an indefeasible title by a

[16] See Dill's *Roman Society From Nero to Marcus Aurelius*, ch. iii.

> charter. He gained a sanction for the Oriental theory of government.[17]

And Professor Seeley is merely summarizing the subsequent history of Christianity when he adds that this characterises the attitude of the Church throughout its entire history.

Such an attitude towards the very spirit of freedom and liberty was not likely to react very favourably on the institution of slavery or on the condition of the slave. And as a matter of fact, the movement towards emancipation in progress under the Pagan Emperors received an almost absolute check under Christian rule. Says Lecky:—

> The Christian Emperors, in A.D. 319 and 326, adverted in two elaborate laws to the subject of the murder of slaves, but beyond reiterating in very emphatic terms the previous enactments, it is not easy to see in what way they improved the condition of the class. . . . The use of torture not intended to kill was in no degree restricted, nor is there anything in the law to make it appear either that the master was liable to punishment, if contrary to his intention his slave succumbed beneath torture, or that Constantine proposed any penalty for excessive cruelty, which did not result in death. . . . For about two hundred years there was an absolute pause in the legislation relating to slavery. . . . Slavery was distinctly and formally recognised by

[17] *Lectures and Essays*, pp. 74-6.

> Christianity, and no religion ever laboured more to encourage a spirit of docility and passive obedience.[18]

So, too, Renan in summing up the attitude of Christianity towards slavery, says:—

> We have seen that the great school of jurisconsults arising from the Antonines, is entirely possessed by this idea, that slavery is an abuse which must be gently suppressed. Christianity never said slavery is an abuse. . . . The idea never came to the Christian doctors to protest against the established fact of slavery. The rights of men were not in any way a Christian affair. St. Paul completely recognised the legitimacy of a master's position. No word occurs in all the ancient Christian literature to preach revolt to the slave, nor to advise the master to manumission, nor even to agitate the problem of public law which has been produced among us concerning slavery. . . . Never is the master Christian who has Christian slaves counselled to free them; it is not forbidden even to use corporal chastisement towards them. If the movement which dates from the Antonines had continued in the second half of the third century, and in the fourth century, the suppression of slavery would

[18] *History of European Morals*, II., pp. 62-6. It is curious to note that in forbidding the killing of slaves that the "Institutes" of the Christian Emperor Justinian gave as a reason for this "It concerns, the public good that no one should misuse his own property." Centuries later (1667), the Virginia Assembly declared the killing of a slave to be only felony, since no one would accuse a man of a desire to destroy his own property. It was property, not persons, that these Christian legislators had in their mind.

have come about as a legal measure, and by redemption money. The ruin of the liberal policy, and the misfortunes of the times, caused all the ground which had been gained to be lost.[19]

[19] *Marcus Aurelius*, p. 346.

III.

Slavery in the Christian Ages

▼ ▼

"CONSIDERING," says Professor Westermarck, "Christianity has been commonly represented as almost the sole cause of the mitigation and final abolition of slavery in Europe, it deserves special notice that the chief improvement in the condition of slaves at Rome took place at so early a period that Christianity could have absolutely no share in it. Nay, for about two hundred years after it was made the official religion of the Empire there was an almost complete pause in the legislation on the subject. . . . Christianity recognised slavery from the beginning. The principle that all men are spiritually equal in Christ does not imply that they should be socially equal in the world. Slavery does not prevent anybody from performing the duties incumbent on a Christian; it does not bar the way to heaven; it is an external affair only, nothing but a name."[20]

"The abrogation of slavery," says Dean Milman,

[20] *Origin and Development of Moral Ideas,* Vol I., pp. 993-4.

"was not contemplated even as a remote possibility. A general enfranchisement seems never to have dawned on the wisest and best of the Christian writers.[21]

"The Church, as such," says the Rev. Dr. T. C. Hall in his elaborate "History of Ethics within Organised Christianity," "never contemplated doing away with slavery, as such, even though Stoicism had denounced it as 'contra mundum.'"[22] Nowhere does the early Church condemn slavery as an institution. Kindness to the slave is frequently recommended, but this was done quite as forcibly, and upon a much broader ground by the pagan writers. It would be indeed nearer the truth to say that the Christians who wrote in favour of the mitigation of the lot of the slave were far more indebted to pagan than to Christian influence. Even in the instances sometimes cited where the slave escaping from a brutal master fled to the Church for protection he was only doing what the slave under paganism had done when he sought refuge in a temple. In either case it meant only the intervention of the priest, Christian or Pagan, to secure the goodwill of the master.

As a matter of fact the Church very early owned slaves, and a Council of Orleans in the middle of the sixth century decreed the perpetuity of servitude

[21] *History of Latin Christianity*, Vol. II., p. 14.

[22] *History of Ethics Within Organized Christianity*, p. 182.

among the descendants of slaves. Even where the Church favoured liberating their slaves, it resolutely refused to liberate the slaves owned by the Church. In the seventh century a Council of Toledo threatened with damnation any bishop who dared to liberate a slave belonging to the Church without compensating the Church.[23] There was even an increase in the number of slaves owned by the Church by the incitement to laymen to will their slaves to her. As a matter of fact, the Church was the last to liberate the slaves she owned.

The mere fact of the perpetuation of slavery under Christian rule is enough to disprove the customary claims put forward by Christian apologists. Sir Henry Maine properly points out that the influences which led to a bettering of the lot of the slave were Pagan rather than Christian in origin,[24] while Finlay sarcastically observes :—

> It has been very generally asserted that we ought to attribute the change (*i.e.*, the extinguishing of slavery) to the influence of the Christian religion. If this be really true, cavallers might observe that so powerful a cause never in any other case produced its effects so tardily.[25]

In the Encyclical Letter to the bishops of Brazil, dated May, 1888, Pope Leo XIII. said it was not pos-

[23] *Westermarck*, Vol. I., p. 699.

[24] See his *Early History of Institutions*, p. 62

[25] *The Byzantine Empire*, p. 261.

sible to deprive the Church of the credit for destroying "this dreadful curse of slavery." The validity of the claim may be gauged from the fact that even in making it the Pope is compelled to enter a number of qualifications. Thus the Church:—

> has deprecated any precipitate action in securing the manumission and liberation of the slaves, because that would have entailed tumults and wrought injury. . . . She taught the slaves to feel that by virtue of the light of holy faith . . . they enjoyed a dignity which placed them above their heathen lords,[26] but they were bound the more strictly by the Author and Founder of their Faith Himself never to set themselves against these, or even to be wanting in the reverence and obedience due to them.[27]

The indisputable fact which stands out is that nowhere is there a clear condemnation of slavery on the part of the early Church. It has been urged that the early Church by one canon forbade the ordination of slaves, and it is assumed that this is an implied condemnation. The plea is negatived by turning to the regulation itself, which plainly bases the prohibition on the ground that "no man was to be defrauded

[26] Pope Leo must have forgotten the decree of the Council of Gangra (fourth century), which pronounced its anathema on anyone who should teach a slave to despise his master on account of religion. This decree was reaffirmed by Pope Hadrian I. in 773.

[27] Letter in Canon Brownlow's *Slavery and Serfdom in Europe*.

of his right under pretence of an ordination,''[28] and was intended to protect the master. This is not a condemnation, but a clear recognition. Lecky says that the number of slaves were greater under Christian than under Pagan rule.[29] H. C. Lea, whose studies in early Church history gives special weight to his testimony, says:—

> The Church held many slaves, and while their treatment was in general sufficiently humane to cause the number to grow by voluntary accretions, yet it had no scruple to assert vigorously their claim to ownership. When the papal church granted a slave to a monastery, the dread anathema, involving eternal perdition, was pronounced against anyone daring to interfere with the gift; and those who were appointed to take charge of the lands and farms of the Church, were specially instructed that it was part of their duty to pursue and recapture fugitive bondsmen.[30]

At a somewhat later date the Venetians were supplying the Mohammedans with slaves, a traffic in which the ecclesiastics and nobility of our own country appear to have taken part—the persons sold being their own serfs. According to Vinogradoff the number of slaves in England at the date of Domesday Book was 25,000.[31] Lecky's opinion as to the increase

[28] See Bingham, *Christian Antiquities*, ii., p. 56.

[29] *European Morals*, ii. 70.

[30] *Studies of Church History*, p. 565.

[31] *English Society in the Eleventh Century*, p. 465.

of the number of slaves seems borne out by the consideration that in the eleventh century, in England, the proportion of slaves in the various counties—resident slaves, be it noted—varied from one in seven to one in twenty-four of the population. A very large trade in the exportation of slaves from Bristol was also organised.[32] More revolting still, slaves were bred for the market as one breeds cattle.[33] One's surprise at this is lessened by remembering that the slave was "a thing not a person, he was classed with his lord's goods and cattle, and seems to have been rated according to a similar schedule, to be disposed of at his lord's pleasure like his oxen and horses."[34] The punishments for slaves were also of a special kind, reviving many of the barbarities prohibited under the Roman Code. In the case of theft, for example :—

> If the thief was a man and a slave, he was to be stoned to death by eighty slaves, and if one missed his mark three times that one was to be whipped three times. If the thief was a female slave, and had stolen from any but her own lord, eighty female slaves were to attend, each bearing a log of wood to pile the fire, and burn the offender to death.[35]

No wonder Mr. Pike remarks of the times that "In

[32] C. M. Andrews, *The Old English Manor*, pp. 182-3.

[33] C. H. Pearson, *The Early and Middle Ages of England*, p. 73.

[34] Andrews, *The Manor*, p. 106.

[35] L. O. Pike, *History of Crime in England*, i., p. 51.

savageness towards slaves and women they have never been surpassed by the wildest tribe in Africa." At any rate, such circumstances enable one to appreciate how much the Christian Church has done either to abolish slavery or to ease the lot of the slave.

The traffic in white slaves lingered on for long after the period just noted. As late as 1547 an Act was passed condemning a "runaway servant" or "idle vagabond" to slavery for two years. In the seventeenth century thousands of Irish—men, women, and children—were seized by the order, or under the licence of the English Government, and sold as slaves for use in the West Indies. In the Calendar of State Papers, under various dates, between 1653-6, the following entries occur: "For a licence to Sir John Clotworthy to transport to America 500 natural Irishmen." A slave dealer, named Sellick, is granted a licence to take 400 children from Ireland for New England and Virginia. Later "1,000 Irish girls and the like number of youths" are sold to the planters in Jamaica.

In Scotland the Parliament passed, in 1606, an Act binding all workmen engaged in coal mines and at salt works to perpetual service. For over a century and a half later whenever coal mines or salt works changed owners those employed were sold with the estates. They were emancipated in 1775 by an Act of the British Parliament, but with certain special conditions that made the Act almost a dead letter. It was not until 1799 that the colliers and salt-workers of Scotland became free men.[36]

Canon Brownlow, in his *Slavery and Serfdom in Europe,* as a means of proving that Christianity abolished slavery, cites various deliveries of Church Councils against the holding of slaves. A very brief examination of these will, however, show that they carry no condemnation of slavery, but only condemn Christian slaves being held by " Heathen " or Jews. In other words, their purpose was a purely religious one. Indeed, Canon Brownlow's own examples prove this to be so. The mediæval monkish orders he cites as having for their purpose the liberation of slaves were engaged in ransoming Christian slaves from the Moors. So long as the master was a Christian no objection was raised to his holding slaves. Good men in the Church favoured the emancipation of slaves, and there are numerous cases of Christians giving freedom to their slaves before or after their death. But this is no more than was the case in ancient Rome, as we have seen; and between this and the prohibition of slavery there is a fundamental distinction.[37]

[36] J. Mackintosh, *History of Civilization in Scotland,* iii., pp. 304-5.

[37] It is illustrative of what has been said that so late as 1677, when the question was raised in an English court, Africans were held to be slaves on the ground of custom, and "as being infidels." See Egglestone's, *The Transit of Civilization,* 1901, p. 304.

Had the Church been against slavery it would have branded it as a wrong, and have set the example of liberating its own slaves. It did neither. Its conscience was only shocked when a Jewish or Heathen master owned Christian slaves. Nay, the Church not only held slaves itself, not only protected others who held slaves, but it thundered against all who should despoil its property by selling or liberating slaves belonging to the Church. The Council of Agatho, 506, considered it unfair to enfranchise the slaves of monasteries, seeing that the monks themselves laboured. The Council of Toledo, 597, stigmatised as robbers those who set free the slaves of the Church without giving an equivalent. The Council of Epaona, 517, prohibited abbots from emancipating the slaves of their monasteries. Slaves were bequeathed to the Church by will, or given as an act of piety, and never was the gift refused. The Church, too, held its slaves to the end. In France, in his day, Voltaire estimated that the Church held between 50,000 and 60,000 slaves.[38]

The whole history of the Christian Church shows that it has never felt itself called upon to fight any social institution, no matter what its character—so long as it favoured the Church. Slavery and serfdom, war, piracy, child labour, have all been in turn sanctioned. The Bishop of the Church has claimed his feudal rights and privileges as heartily as the mediæval

[38] Art. "Slavery," *Philosophical Dictionary*.

lord, and retained them longest. Its relation to slavery is, in fact, an epitome of its attitude towards social problems in general. It has taken existing institutions and, so long as they did not oppose the Church, given them its blessing. It gave a recreated slave trade in modern times the same support it gave to the ancient traffic. Small wonder it is that when, as Mr. Hobhouse says, the Christian world came into direct contact with the black races there was "no moral force at hand to resist the natural result."[39] How could there be in a society which had been for so long subject to the powerful influence of the Christian Church?

It may serve as a kind of footnote to what has been said to take one country where the influence of Christianity has been dominant for a longer period than anywhere else in the world, and where it has encountered fewer anti-Christian influences than any other country in the world. Biblical influence in Abyssinia is said to have been continuous from 982 B.C. up till to-day. The establishment of Christianity there dates from the fourth century. Since then the Christian religion enters into the national life in a way that cannot easily be realised by a people like ourselves with whom for hundreds of years genuine Christianity has been prevented exercising its full power by other and more civilised factors. The

[39] *Morals in Evolution*, i., 317.

most powerful institution in the country, next to the king and his government, is the Church. If there is a country on the face of the earth where the Christian religion is secure and unquestioned, where non-Christian influences are at their lowest point, where anti-Christian ones are unknown, and consequently where the alleged anti-slavery tendencies could have had freest expression, it is Abyssinia. What are the facts?

In 1929 Lady Kathleen Simon published a book, "Slavery," dealing with the slave trade of the world. The facts therein related concerning Abyssinia are not unknown to those who have enquired into the matter. I select the book because it is the most recent, and is written by one who has no bias against Christianity. Probably the bias is on the other side.

There is one authoritative document referred to by Lady Simon that is worth a word in passing. In 1922, the League of Nations ordered an enquiry into the slave trade of Abyssinia. The head of the Commission was Lord Lugard, a man of admitted ability and judgment. The report was prepared, and submitted to the League. It is said to have been, as one would have expected, a very able document. But the report has never been published. Why? Is it because Abyssinia, being a Christian country, it was thought inadvisable to call attention to this slave trading state? Knowing what one does of the methods of suppression practised by the Christian Churches one would not be surprised to find this to be the correct explanation. At any rate, the fact is there.

From Lady Simon's work I take the following summary of the situation, not a single statement having been questioned since the publication of the work. The population of Abyssinia is at least ten millions, and of this population not less than one-fifth, probably more, are slaves. Lord Lugard has pointed out that slavery is so rooted in Abyssinian life that any attempt to uproot it must involve a complete change in the life of the people. More than that it is pointed out that slave-owning is "an integral part of the religion of the country." Also that opposition to the abolition of slavery,

> comes principally from the priesthood which considers itself the guardian of the Mosaic law, and regards slavery as an institution ordered by Jehovah.

Slave raids are constant, raids for young men who are required for various purposes, and young girls who are sold for Arabian harems. These raids are accompanied with all the brutalities and consequences that many people believe belonged to a long gone past. That this is not the case will be seen from the following. Writing in the *Westminster Gazette*, in January, 1922, one of our own officers, Major Darley, tells of a district which on his first visit was prosperous with a dense population. Of this area, he says, as a result of slave raids,

> To-day it is possible to march through this district for days without meeting a single human being. . . . The people who should be sowing and reaping are either dead or slaves in the capital. The whole countryside is abandoned to the jackals and the hyaenas.

From his own personal experience of the nature of these raids, Major Darley says that on the trail of these slave processions he has

> counted the dead and dying bodies of more than fifty captives who have dropped by the roadside. For on such journeys there is no commissariat compartment department, and those who carry no food can hope only for a merciful spear, since the alternative is death by thirst or by the teeth and talons of wild beasts.

This story, says Lady Simon, is the tale told by every man and woman who has come into intimate contact with Abyssinian life. Even the present King received, while Prince Regent, a present of 140 slaves, most of whom were children of both sexes, although a few were women with babies at the breast. Major Darley tells us that "Gangs of slaves, marching in misery, the men chained together in rows, and the women and children dragging themselves along beside the main body, can be seen by any traveller in Southern Abyssinia to-day. Some of these slaves are captured on Abyssinian territory, others in British East Africa, others in the Anglo-Egyptian Soudan."

The slave trade in Abyssinia is open, its horrors are

well known, and it is supported by the Christian Church of the country. It is alleged that it is the religious prejudice that will be the strongest obstacle in the way of slavery being accepted.

Such is slavery in the most Christian country in the world to-day, the country which has the longest Christian history of any nation in the world. Its existence helps us to realise the value of the statement that the power of Christianity in the world destroyed the slave trade. Slavery flourishes in the oldest of Christian countries in the world, backed up by the Church, the Old Bible and the New Testament. It has all the horrors, all the brutalities, all the degradations of the slave trade at its worst. Such is Christian Abyssinia, and such, but for the saving grace of secular civilisation, would be the rest of the world.

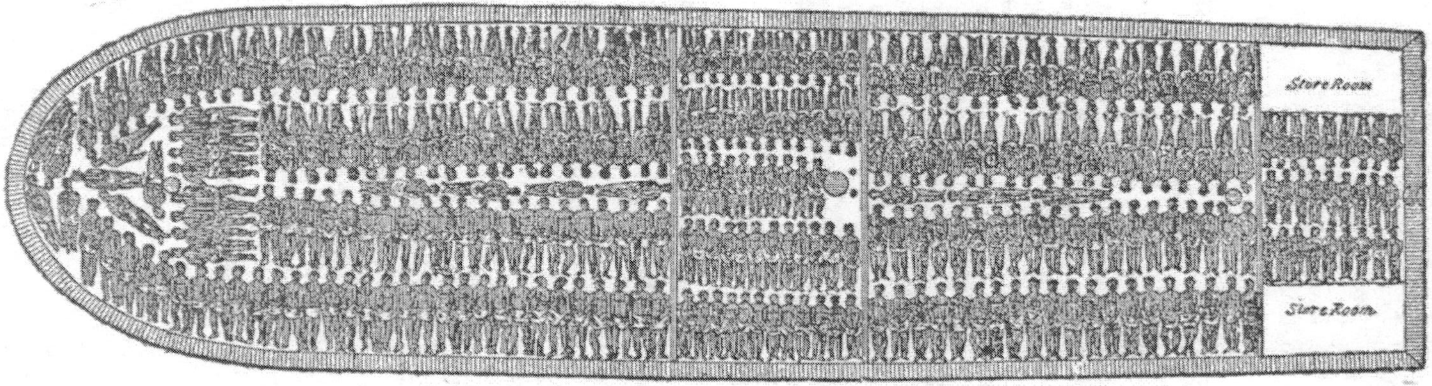

THE SLAVE-SHIP "BROOKES"—MAIN DECK—BERTHING PLAN (*see page* 51).

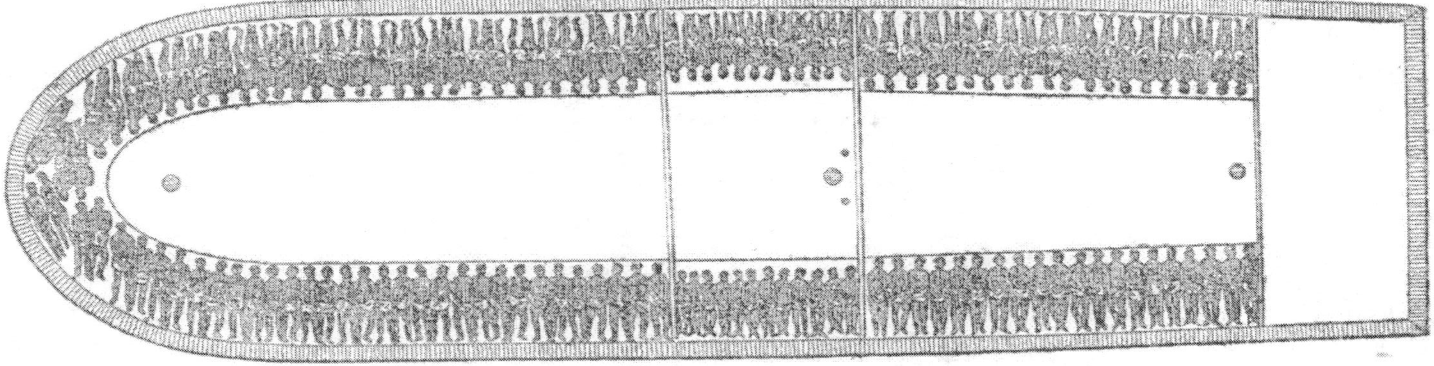

THE SLAVE-SHIP "BROOKES"—PLATFORM BETWEEN DECKS (*see page* 51).

IV.

The English Slave Trade

◆ ◆

THE peculiar and damning fact in the history of slavery—so far as the Christian Church is concerned—is this. The history of slavery divides itself into two parts. There is first of all the ancient slave system, which was common to all countries, and may be said to have been almost an inevitable phase of social evolution. That died out, to be replaced by serfdom, to be replaced in turn by other forms of labour. So far, no responsibility for slavery attaches to the Christian Church. The most that can be said is that it accepted and endorsed it. But we have another slave system to deal with. This took its rise in Christian times. It was created by Christians, it was continued by Christians, it was in some respects more barbarous than anything the world had yet seen, and its worst features were to be witnessed in countries that were most ostentatious in their parade of Christianity. It is this that provides the final and unanswerable indictment of the Christian Church.

Some few African slaves appear to have been imported into Europe during the early part of the fifteenth century, but nothing in the nature of a systematic traffic existed. This began with the conquest of the twin-empires of Mexico and Peru by the Spaniards. Acting under the authority of the Church, South America was to experience the full benefits of Christian civilisation. In Spain, the Church was in process of wiping out one civilisation. In South America it deliberately destroyed another civilisation that was superior in many respects to anything that existed in Christian Europe. Forced to labour in the mines, the native Mexicans and Peruvians were dying like flies. In 1517, Bartolome de las Casas, Bishop of Chiapa, proposed, it is suggested out of good nature and in the hope of benefiting the natives, that each Spanish gentleman should be permitted to import twelve negro slaves.[40] The advice of the Bishop was adopted. The King gave a patent to one of his favourites, authorising him to import 4,000 negroes annually to Hispaniola, Cuba, Jamaica, and Porto Rica. This patent was soon sold to the Genoese, who shared it with the Portuguese. There is no reason, however, to believe that any limit was in practice placed on the number imported, and all the nations of Europe were soon engaged in the traffic. It should be added that, accord-

[40] It is said that in fifteen years the Spaniards of Hispaniola had reduced the natives from one million to sixty thousand (Ingram, *History of Slavery*, pp. 143-4).

ing to Livingstone, slavery was unknown to the Africans until it was introduced by Christians—the Portuguese.[41]

The first Englishman of note to engage in the traffic was the celebrated John Hawkins, afterwards knighted by Elizabeth and appointed Treasurer to the Navy. Froude calls him "a peculiarly characteristic figure," and he certainly presents that blending of piracy and piety, rascality and religion, so common in the days of Elizabeth and not altogether unknown in ours. Hawkins appears to have had his eye for a long time on the slave trade as a very lucrative business, and as the Spaniards claimed a practical monopoly, patriotic feeling—the desire to break down the Spanish claim—went, as is again not unusual, with profit. At any rate, after a reconnoitering trip, Hawkins returned to England and fitted out an expedition of five vessels, to

[41] *Expedition to the Zambesi,* p. 240. Says Lecky: Scarcely anyone seems to have regarded the trade as wrong. According to the popular sentiment of Christendom there was such an amazing, I might almost say general, difference between those who were Christians and those who were not, that to apply to the latter the principles that were applied to the former, would have been deemed a glaring paradox. If the condition of the negroes in this world was altered for the worse, it was felt that their prospects in the next were greatly improved. Besides, it was remembered that, shortly after the deluge, Ham had behaved disrespectfully to his drunken father, and it was believed by many that the Almighty had, in consequence, ordained negro slavery" (*History of Rationalism,* ii. 333-4). Thus the state of opinion on the topic of human brotherhood was actually at a lower level than it was in the old Roman Empire.

which were later added another three. In this venture, the Earl of Leicester, the Earl of Pembroke, and others took shares. So did Queen Elizabeth. She lent the ship *Jesus,* and Hawkins drew up rules for his men, the two first of which ran: "Serve God daily," and "Love one another." The piety of the expedition was beyond reproach. So was its practice, as we read that finding the natives of Cape Verd to be of "a nature very gentle and loving," and "more civil than any others," Hawkins prepared to kidnap a number of them. After sailing for some time, "burning and spoiling," he landed in the Spanish American settlements and compelled the Colonists to purchase the slaves at his own price. Quite fittingly Hawkins was granted a coat of arms consisting of "a demi-Moor in his proper colours, bound and captive," as a token of the new trade he had opened to Englishmen.[42]

The English slave trade remained for a long time in the hands of licensed companies; it was not until the reign of William and Mary that it was thrown open to all. One of our wars was, indeed, caused through a slave treaty. By the Treaty of Utrecht, the asiento or contract for supplying the South American Colonies with 4,800 slaves annually had passed from the Dutch to the French, and from the French to the British.

[42] See Ingram's *History of Slavery,* pp. 145-7, and Froude's *English Seamen of the Sixteenth Century,* ch. 2.

When the contract came to an end in 1739, Philip V. declared his intention to revoke the asiento, and popular feeling ran so high that Sir Robert Walpole was forced to declare war. Between 1680 and 1700, says Ingram, 140,000 negroes were imported by the English African Company, and about 160,000 more by private traders. Between 1700 and 1786, as many as 610,000 were transported to Jamaica alone.[42a] In the hundred years ending 1776, the English carried into the Spanish, French, and English Colonies three million slaves.[43] Large numbers were required to keep up the supply, owing to the many who died during the passage. They—

> were chained to each other hand and foot, and stored so close that they were not allowed above a foot and a half for each in breadth. Thus, crammed together like herrings in a barrel, they contracted putrid and fatal disorders, so that they who came to inspect them in the morning had occasionally to pick dead slaves out of their rows and to unchain their

[42a] In a return presented to Parliament in 1770, the following figures are given as to sales by the various European Countries: French 20,000, Portugese 10,000, Dutch 4,000, Danes 2,000, and England 38,000. More than half of the European trade was thus being done by Britain. Writing under date of February 25, 1750, Horace Walpole says: "We have been sitting this fortnight on the African Company. We, the British Senate, that bulwark of Protestant Christianity, have this fortnight been considering methods to make more effectual the horrid traffic of selling negroes. It has appeared to us that six and forty thousand of these wretches are sold every year to our plantations alone."

[43] Lecky, *History of England*, vol. ii., pp. 244-5.

carcases from the bodies of their wretched fellow-sufferers to whom they had been fastened.

Exclusive of the slaves who died before leaving Africa, not more than fifty out of every hundred lived to work on the plantations. It is calculated that although between 1690 and 1820 no less than 800,000 negroes had been imported to Jamaica, yet, at the latter date, only 340,000 were on the island.[44] Could anything connected with Roman slavery compare with this?

The three chief centres for the British slave trade in England were Bristol, Liverpool, and London. Gradually Bristol, always a city of unquestioned piety, gained on the Metropolis. At the commencement of the eighteenth century, London had over one hundred vessels engaged in the trade; about five years later it had only fifty, and a little later thirty. On the other hand, the number of vessels that left Bristol annually for the slave coast, from 1701 to 1732, averaged sixty. But a new rival to Bristol declared itself in Liverpool, and a study of the traffic from that port may serve as a picture of the whole.

The first slave vessel that left the Mersey in 1709 carried only fifteen slaves from Africa to the West Indies. But the profits—judging from the rapid increase in the traffic—must have been very great, for by 1714, only five years later, more than half the vessels engaged in the trade belonged to Liverpool, and it was

[44] Ingram, p. 153.

calculated that Liverpool ships imported three-sevenths of all the slaves carried by Europeans. In 1795, one-fourth of the ships belonging to the port of Liverpool were engaged in the slave trade, the actual increase being from 15 ships in 1730, to 136 in 1792. The traffic underwent a still greater increase prior to its abolition. From January, 1806, to May, 1807, no less than 185 Liverpool owned slave vessels left Africa with a slave-carrying capacity of nearly 50,000.[45]

The trade was attractive on account of its huge profits. The actual cost of a slave on the West Coast of Africa—the cost, that is, to secure; because a very large part of the business was pure kidnapping—ranged from £15 to £35. The selling price would be anything from £50 to £100, depending upon the age, health, and general condition of the "goods." The net gain on the slave traffic appears to have been upward of 60 per cent. In 1796, Liverpool returned a net profit of £298,462 sterling, and during eleven years the gains on 303,737 slaves was £2,361,455 6s. 1d., or, on an average, £214,677 15s. 1d. per annum. It is small wonder that G. F. Cooke, the tragedian, on being hissed by a Liverpool audience, retorted: "I have not come here to be insulted by a

[45] These and most of the following statements concerning the Liverpool slave trade are taken from a work entitled *Liverpool and Slavery*, by A Genuine "Dicky Sam," Liverpool, 1884.

set of wretches, of which every brick in your infernal town has been cemented by an African's blood."

At the commencement of the British slave trade there does not appear to have been any regulations concerning the carrying of slaves. It was, on the face of it, to the owner's interest to lose as few slaves as possible by death, and to get them to their journey's end in as good a condition as possible. But the obviously sensible course in such matters does not appear to have been always—perhaps not generally—followed, and legislation on the subject appears. A ship of 300 tons was allowed to carry 500 slaves, with a crew of 50. But these regulations seem to have been only nominal. Thus the work from which I am quoting gives the actual dimensions of a famous slave ship, the *Brookes*. The vessel was of 297 tons, and was allowed to carry 450 persons. As a matter of fact, she had carried 351 men, 127 women, 90 boys, and 41 girls—a total of 609. The length of the lower deck, on which the slaves were carried, was only 100 ft., and in this space the slaves were packed without regard for health or decency. It was customary to allow 6 ft. by 1 ft. 4 in. for a man, 6 ft. by 1 ft. 4in. for a woman, 5 ft. by 1 ft. 2 in. for a boy, and 4 ft. 6 in. by 1 ft. for a girl. Had they been measured for coffins, not much less space could have been allowed; and coffins these ships often were. In fact, in some cases it was only possible for the slaves to lie down to sleep by arranging them alternately head to feet.

So close were they, one could not walk without treading on them; but they were only slaves. One kind-hearted sailor, when passing over them, would remove his shoes, so as not to hurt them. So close and foul was the stench arising from the negroes, they have been known to be put down the hold strong and healthy at night, and to have been dead in the morning. A trader stated that, after remaining ten minutes in the hold, his shirt was as wet as if it had been in a bucket of water.

In the case of one Liverpool ship, the *Thomas*, carrying 630 slaves, 100 died on the voyage; but as the remaining 530 sold at Jamaica at £60 per head, the owners were, doubtless, well satisfied with the trip. In some cases, however, the mortality was much greater—running to fifty out of every hundred. All the slaves were not sold abroad; some were disposed of in Liverpool. Thus, an old paper, *Liverpool Chronicle*, advertises :—

> A fine negro boy, to be sold by auction. He is 11 years of age; the auction will take place at the Merchant's Coffee House, Old Church Yard. By order of Mr. Thomas Yates, who hath imported him from Bonney.

The *Liverpool Advertiser* of 1765 also announces :—

> To be sold by auction, at George's Coffee House,

betwixt the hours of six and eight o'clock, a very fine negro girl, about 8 years of age; very healthy.

Also, under date of September 8, 1766 :—

To be sold, at the Exchange Coffee House, Walter Street, at one o'clock precisely, eleven negroes, imported per the *Angola*.

In the colonial papers long lists of runaway slaves were advertised, most of them branded like so many cattle. The following will serve as specimens: "Robert, R.P. on each cheek, and Kingston, marked *Yorke* on each shoulder and breast." Another is branded with "a cattle mark." "An old woman with her two sons and two daughters, one of them big with child." One man is to be recognised by his having had "both ears cropt"; another by having had "his nose and ears cut off." Another advertisement runs, "Escaped on Sunday last with a chain and collar round his neck, a negro man, marked T.Y." Another, after carefully describing a runaway slave girl, concludes by saying, "Whoever will apprehend the said wench, alive or dead, will receive two moidores reward from Joseph Charles Howard."

Most of the old Liverpool families were more or less steeped in the slave trade, and their enterprise made Liverpool the greatest slave town in Europe. Some of its "brands" were famous, particularly that of "D.D." Many of the slaves were sold openly on the Custom House steps, and the announcements of the sale and the descriptions of the slaves differs in no respect from those of cattle. Indeed, they were so much cattle. They were branded exactly as cattle are branded. The slave was made to kneel down, and the red-hot branding-iron was placed on the bare flesh—usually on the buttock. No one, for a long time, seems to have seen anything unusual or cruel in this. It was just part of a commercial transaction. The ship in which Hawkins commenced the trade was named the *Jesus;* Whitefield was not only a slave-owner himself, but argued strongly for the introduction of slaves into Georgia; the Society for the Propagation of the Gospel was a large slave-owner; Nelson, writing to a friend in Jamaica, under date of June 10, 1805, declared himself a firm friend of the colonial system, and said he was prepared to defend it against the "damnable and cursed doctrine of Wilberforce and his hypocritical allies." (*Monthly Repository,* 1807, p. 203.) Lord Dartmouth, one of the most religious statesmen of the century, declared that we could not allow the Colonies to check or discourage in any degree a traffic so beneficial to the nation; and Newton, the evangelist, who was at one time the captain of a slave-ship, said that "he never knew sweeter or more frequent hours of divine communion than on his two last voyages to Guinea."[46] And, what with the horrors

[46] Cited in article in *Edinburgh Review,* January, 1901. P. 3.

of the passage on board ship, and the treatment afterwards, it may safely be said that the slave trade as organised by Christian merchants far outdid, in deliberate cruelty, anything that ancient times could show.

I have referred to the slave-ship *Thomas*. Here is a copy of one of the bills of lading :—

> Shipped by the grace of God in good order, and well conditioned, by James Dodd, in and upon the good ship "Thomas," master under God for this present voyage, Captain Peter Roberts, and now at anchor at Calabar, and by God's grace bound for Jamaica, with 630 slaves, men and women, branded D.D., and numbered in the margin 31 D.D., and are to be delivered in good state, and well conditioned, at the port of Kingston (the dangers of the seas and mortality alone excepted) unto Messrs. Broughton & Smith. In witness whereof the master and purser of the ship "Thomas" hath affirmed to this bill of lading, and God send the good ship to her destined port in safety, Amen. October 31st, 1767.

This unctuous piety was made to cover the most villainous traffic that the world has ever seen. African villages were burned, and the inhabitants—men, women, and children—marched to the coast, branded, pushed into the holds, and carried away to Kingston or elsewhere for sale. Parties of negroes were invited on board ships to trade, and were seized and made slaves. Slaves that fell sick were so much useless lumber, and were often thrown overboard out of hand. Some attempt to keep them in health was made by bringing them out of the hold in batches and compelling them to jump about the decks under the persuasive influence of a cat-o'-nine-tails. The deaths of a few slaves more or less, however, roused no comments so long as the dividends remained high.[47]

In the latter half of the eighteenth century, voices began to be raised, first for the humanising of the traffic, and later for its abolition. But as late as the Parliamentary election of 1761 the speeches of all the political candidates were unanimously in favour of resisting attempts to restrict the trade in "black ivory." Had there been a readiness to permit an increase of regulations concerning the slave traffic, it is possible that it might have continued for more years than was actually the case. But resistance to reform paved the way for abolition, although to the last, Liverpool put up a strong fight for its perpetuation. As late as 1790, in the Parliamentary election, the Gascoyne party enforced their claims in the following doggerel:—

Be true to the man who stood to his trust,

[47] During the hearing of a case for insurance, the following facts were brought out. A slave-ship, with 442 slaves, was bound from Guinea to Jamaica. Sixty of the slaves died from overcrowding. The captain, being short of water, threw ninety-six more overboard. Afterwards, twenty-six more were drowned. Ten drowned themselves in despair. Yet the ship reached port before the water was exhausted.—Goldwin Smith, *The United Kingdom: a Political History*, ii., p. 247.

Remember our real situation we must;
When our African business was near at an end,
Remember, my lads, 'twas Gascoyne was our friend;
If our slave trade had gone, there's an end to our lives,
Beggars all we must be, our children and wives;
No ships from our ports their proud sails e'er would spread,
And our streets grown with grass, where the cows might be fed.

The ruin of Liverpool was freely predicted if the slave traffic was to be abolished. When the Bill for its abolition was finally before Parliament a petition was drawn up, signed by over 2,000 Liverpool merchants and citizens, demanding the withdrawal of the measure. The petition was signed by no less than eight ex-Mayors of Liverpool, and set forth :—

That many of your petitioners having, under the protection of the legislature, embarked a considerable part of their property in that trade, will be very materially injured if the said Bill should pass into law. That such abolition, in your petitioners' judgment, would not only be a great detriment to the town of Liverpool, but in its consequences produce great distress to the extensive manufactures of the County of Lancaster, and to many of the other rich, opulent, and industrious manufacturing towns in the kingdom, and would in no way answer the benevolent purposes of humanity, but only serve to remove the advantages of this trade to foreign States. Your petitioners, therefore, most humbly pray that the said Bill may not pass into law, and that they may be heard by their Counsel at your Lordships' bar.

As a matter of fact, the number of ships entering and leaving Liverpool fell off considerably with the abolition of the slave trade, and dock dues fell by about a third. In a few years, however, outlets were found in other directions, and the port continued to grow steadily. But it must be recorded as an indication of the state of opinion in Liverpool, that when, in 1788, the Society for the Abolition of the Slave Trade published its list of members, only two Liverpool names were found in it—William Rathbone and Dr. Binns.

As in America at a later date, the defenders of the traffic fell back upon religion and the Bible as authority for slave dealing. It was argued that the Bible had instituted slavery, and whatever abuses might occur in particular cases could not be urged against the institution. This, it must be remembered, was the line taken by W. E. Gladstone, in his first address to the electors of Newark. The Society for the Propagation of the Gospel possessed numerous slaves of its own, and when, in 1783, Bishop Porteous urged giving them instruction, the recommendation was absolutely declined.[48]

Foremost amongst those who gained fame in Liver-

[48] Lecky, *History of England in the Eighteenth Century*, vol. ii., p. 249.

pool as a champion of slavery was the Rev. Raymond Harris, a clergyman of the Church of England. In 1788 he published a pamphlet with the title, " Scriptural Researches of the Licitness of the Slave Trade, showing its conformity with the principles of Natural and Revealed Religion, delineated in the sacred writings of the Word of God." He points out that slavery was sanctioned by God, and so remains unless explicitly cancelled. He draws a number of illustrations from the Bible, and concludes that those who do not believe the slave trade to be a " licit " occupation really do not believe their Bibles. There were other clerical champions of the trade, and it is worth while noting that the Rev. John Newton, friend of Cowper, author of the *Olney Hymns,* and Rector of St. Mary's, Woolnoth, actually commanded a slave-ship during the time he was studying for the ministry.

In 1776, the question was raised in the House of Commons by Mr. David Hartley, M.P. for Hull. His motion was, however, defeated. In 1789 Pitt introduced a Bill against the African Slave Trade, which was followed with one by Wilberforce. The first motion by Wilberforce was rejected by 163 votes to 88. Three times it met with the same fate, and when it had passed the Lower and went to the Upper House it was rejected on an equal number of occasions. One member of the House of Commons, Mr. Stanley, said it appeared to him " to be the intention of Providence that one set of men should always be slaves to another." The incapacity of Parliament to deal with the matter was generally asserted. General Gascoigne fell back upon the Bible in opposing the measure, and argued for slavery on the ground that it opened up to the negro the blessing of Christianity. Later, when Clarkson's Bill for the Abolition of the Slave Trade was before the House of Lords, Lord Thurlow denounced the measure as contrary to the spirit of the Bible. "Slavery," he said, "had flourished in the early ages when men communed with God, and to attack its legality was an insidious and heretical attack on the principles of religion." It is only due to the Quakers to say that alone, among the Christian sects, they made a stand against slavery. In 1727, they declared it to be "not commendable or allowed," and in 1761 excluded from the Society all who took part in it. But the Quakers have always been a small and "peculiar" body of believers. It was left for anti-Christian, revolutionary France to set the example to the rest of Europe by being the first to decree the freedom of the slaves in its colonies.

V.

American Slavery

WHEN we turn from Europe to America we have, in the main, a repetition of the story we have been relating. Nevertheless, it is imperative to our purpose that the story of the relations of American Christianity to the slave trade shall be told in some detail.

It does not appear that slavery was known in North America prior to the settlement in that country by Europeans. It is unlikely that slavery should have existed, seeing that the inhabitants consisted of nomadic tribes, with whom slavery would not have been a very convenient or profitable institution. But the seventeenth century Christian settlers took slavery with them as part of the established order of things, and would have agreed with the great Catholic Bishop Bossuet that "to condemn slavery was to condemn the Holy Ghost." Among the upholders of slavery in America was George Whitefield, the great Methodist preacher.[49] On some points, the ideas of

[49] Lecky, *History of England,* vol. ii., p. 248.

Christians on the subject appear to have undergone a change for the worse in their new environment. There did exist in Europe, as we have seen, a feeling that while Christians might own non-Christian slaves, it was better they should not make slaves of those who were Christians. But in 1667 the Virginia Assembly decreed that conversion and baptism should not operate to set the slave free.[50] It was probably the case here as in New England of the same period, of which one writer says:—

> The law of the Old Testament was the law of the New England colonist at this period, and, therefore, slavery in itself and the enslavement of women and children, after the total destruction of their male enemies, who were the enemies of the Lord, after the manner of the Israelites of old, was a duty.[51]

From time to time, it is true, there were protests raised against the holding of slaves, but, always, religious arguments were advanced for the practice.[52] But at the end of the eighteenth and the beginning of the nineteenth century the development of English

[50] Fisher's *Colonial Era in America*, p. 57.

[51] J. Douglas, *New England and New France*, p. 293. Of Boston, writing in 1718, when the trade in slaves had assumed great proportions, and when slaves were classed with cattle, Judge Sewell says: "I essayed to prevent the Indians being rated with horses and hogs, but could not prevail" (cited by Douglas, p. 296).

[52] A number of these may be seen in the series of original documents printed in Hart's *American History Told by Contemporaries*. 4 vols. 1898.

manufactures stimulated the demand for cotton, and the economic advantages of slavery strangled, for a time, emancipatory ideas. And as the importation of negroes had by that time almost ceased, a new occupation manifested itself, that of breeding slaves for the market, much as one breeds cattle. In 1840, Virginia exported no less than 40,000 slaves. Virginia was the chief place for breeding, which contained what were virtually a number of stud farms. Lord Macaulay, in a speech delivered before the House of Commons on February 26, 1845, said:—

> The slave States of the Union are divided into two classes, the breeding States, where the human beasts of burden increase and multiply and become strong for labour, and the sugar and cotton States to which these beasts of burden are sent to be worked to death. Bad enough it is that civilized man should sail to an uncivilized quarter of the world where slavery exists, should there buy wretched barbarians, and should carry them away to labour in a distant land; bad enough! But that a civilized man, a baptised man, a man proud of being a citizen of a free State, a man frequenting a Christian Church, should breed slaves for exportation, and, if the whole horrible truth must be told, should even beget slaves for exportation, should see children, sometimes his own children, gambolling from infancy, should watch their growth, should become familiar with their faces, and should sell them for four or five hundred dollars a head, and send them to lead in a remote country a life which is a lingering

death, a life about which the best thing that can be said is that it is sure to be short; this does, I own, excite a horror exceeding even the horror excited by that slave trade which is the curse of the African coast. And mark; I am speaking of a trade as regular as the trade in pigs between Dublin and Liverpool, or as the trade in coals between the Tyne and the Thames.

Could any Christian say anything that is essentially worse than this of the slavery that existed in Pagan times, eighteen centuries earlier? In sheer brutality the Christian slave system of America outdid anything known to the ancient world. "The policy of the slaveholder," says Dr. W. E. B. Du Bois, "was to kill off the negroes by overwork and buy more." The mortality may be inferred from some figures given by Dr. Du Bois. It is calculated that 2,750,000 slaves were imported in the seventeenth century, and 7,000,000 in the eighteenth.[53] Nevertheless, and notwithstanding their normally rapid birth-rate, in 1790 the number of slaves in America totalled no more than 697,897.[54] Of this number, all but about 40,000 were in the Southern States. The members and ministers of the orthodox Churches in the South are said to have owned no less than 660,000 slaves.

We are not here concerned with the history of the slave from the political and economic side. That the

[53] *Inter-Racial Problems*, 1911, p. 349.

[54] Fiske, *Critical Period of American History*, p. 266.

latter is of importance is clear. Indeed, the divisions of American opinion into slavery and anti-slavery was largely determined by the latter factor. The Southern States were dependent upon a plentiful supply of cheap labour, and slavery provided this. On the other hand, the North was not under this need, and Abolitionist opinion made headway. In our country, it may be noted, that Abolitionist opinion was greatly strengthened and enlarged by the growing recognition that slave labour was really less economically profitable than free labour. In this respect, Finlay's statement that no Christian State has ever abolished slavery while it was found to be economically profitable, may be taken as a general expression of the truth.

What we are concerned with is the attitude of the Christian Churches towards the institution of slavery. And the answer to that is well given in the words of William Lloyd Garrison. His biographers say that he "found the religious press, without regard to denomination, filled with apologies for sin and sinners of the worst class." American Christianity "is the main pillar of American slavery." Slaveholders were vouched for as "Christians, sincere followers of the Lord Jesus." And Garrison himself says:—

> It is a fact, alike indisputable and shameful, that the Christianity of the nineteenth century is preached and professed by those who hold their brethren in bondage as brute beasts! And so entirely polluted

> has the Church become, that it has not moral power enough to excommunicate a member who is guilty of man-stealing. Whether it be Unitarian or Orthodox, Baptist or Methodist, Universalist or Episcopal, Roman Catholic or Christian, it is full of innocent blood. . . . At the South, slaves and slaveholders, the masters and their victims, make up the *Christian* Church. The Churches of the North partake of the guilt of oppression, inasmuch as they are in full communion with those of the South.[55]

Speaking generally, the only Christian body in America that consistently condemned slavery was the Quakers; but even these, while favourable to emancipation, kept aloof from the Abolitionists.[56] It was left for Thomas Paine to sound the first clear and effective note on the subject. His article on "Justice and Humanity," demanding emancipation, was published in March, 1775.[57] The article attracted considerable attention, and thirty-five days later led to the establishment of an American Anti-Slavery Society. And it is only fitting that the campaign against slavery thus

[55] *William Lloyd Garrison.* By his Children. Vol. I., pp. 479-80.

[56] *William Lloyd Garrison,* ii., 78.

[57] Republished in Conway's edition of *Works,* vol. i. Mr. Conway also asserts that Paine drafted the Yennsylvania Act
Conway also asserts that Paine drafted the Pennsylvania Act
of its kind in Christendom.

inaugurated should have been triumphantly closed by Abraham Lincoln, another Freethinker.[58]

Many Christians, of course, whose humanity got the better of their theology, and who ignored the opposition of the Churches, stood for emancipation, but, in the main, the Churches as a whole, and the overwhelming majority of Christians, saw nothing unchristian or radically wrong in slave-owning. Something of the nature of the institution has already been indicated. It has likewise been said that alone in the history of slavery Christians aimed at an enslavement of the

[58] Many attempts have been made to prove that Lincoln was a Christian, but the testimony of those who knew him runs in quite the opposite direction. Thus, W. H. Lamon, in his *Life,* points out that when, in 1846, during a contested election, he was accused of being an "Infidel," and was asked to deny the charge, Lincoln replied that he would "die first." Mr. Lamon says: "The community in which he lived was a community of Freethinkers . . . and it was no secret, nor has it been a secret since, that Mr. Lincoln agreed with the majority of his associates in denying to the Bible the authority of divine revelation" (p. 137). "He had written a book—now lost—proving (*a*) that the Bible was not God's revelation, (*b*) Jesus was not the son of God" (p. 158). "Mr. Lincoln was never a member of any Church" (p. 486). "When he went to church, he went to mock, and came away to mimic" (p. 487). Pages 487-500 contain the testimonies of friends as to Lincoln's religious views, from which I take the following:—The Hon. J. T. Stuart: "I knew Mr. Lincoln when he first came here, and for years afterwards. He was an avowed and open infidel, sometimes bordered on Atheism. Lincoln went further against Christianity than any man I ever heard." Mr. Hernden—his law partner—says: "As to Mr. Lincoln's views, he was an infidel." And his wife said: "Mr. Lincoln had no hope and no faith, in the usual acceptance of these terms."

mind of the slave by making his education a penal offence. And the more material side of it is indicated by a law of Louisiana, passed in 1806, which stipulated that a slave shall have at least two-and-a-half hours' rest out of each twenty-four.[59]

In old Rome, as we have seen, encouragement was given to acts of manumission. In Christian America the reverse policy was followed. By the Statutes of North Carolina (1836-7) emancipation was only given to a slave on condition that he or she left the State within ninety days. By the Civil Code of Louisiana (1852) a liberated slave was to be sent out of the State. It was also stated in a Statute of Louisiana that—

> free people of colour ought never to insult or strike white people, nor presume to conceive themselves equal to the whites; but, on the contrary, they ought to yield to them on every occasion, and never speak or answer them but with respect, under the penalty of imprisonment, according to the nature of the offence (cited by Westermarck, *Moral Ideas,* vol. i., p. 714).

In Mississippi a negro was legally punished with thirty-five lashes if he exercised the functions of a minister of the Gospel.

Mr. Weld, in his *American Slavery as It Is,* describes the condition of the slaves as follows:—

They are overworked, underfed, wretchedly clad

[59] See article in *Westminster Review* for 1853, p. 143.

and lodged, and have insufficient sleep; they are often made to wear round their necks iron collars armed with prongs, to drag heavy chains and weights at their feet while working in the fields. . . . They are frequently flogged with terrible severity, have red pepper rubbed into their lacerated flesh, and hot brine, spirits of turpentine, etc., poured over the gashes to increase the torture. . . . Their ears are often cut off, their eyes knocked out, their bones broken, their flesh branded with hot irons. . . . We shall show, not merely that such deeds are committed, but that they are frequent; not done in corners, but before the sun . . . perpetrated by magistrates, by professors of religion, by preachers of the Gospels, by governors of States, by gentlemen of standing, and by delicate females moving in the highest circles of society.

The advertisements for runaway slaves are equally illuminating, mixed up as they are with advertisements of lost or stolen cattle. We have space for but a few specimens. From the *Annual Report of the American Anti-Slavery Society for* 1837, I take the following specimens reprinted from American papers:—

"There was committed to the gaol of Covington County a negro man "who says his name is Josiah . . . is five feet eight inches high . . . his back very much scarred with the whip, and branded (M) on the thigh and hips in three or four places."

"200 Dollars Reward—Ran away from the subscriber a certain negro man named Ben. . . . Also one other negro by the name of Rigdon. . . . I will give the reward of one hundred dollars for each of the above negroes to be delivered to me, or confined in the jail of Lenoir or Jones County, or for the killing of them so that I can see them."

The following when placed in juxtaposition are interesting:—

"Run away, the 24 of last month . . . A Mulatto. . . . Whoever takes up and secures said fellow so that his Master may have him again, shall have forty shillings reward and reasonable charges paid."

"Strayed or stolen on the 15th of April. . . . A black horse about 15 hands high. . . . Whoever brings the said horse to the subscribers shall have ten shillings reward and reasonable charges paid." [60]

Perhaps one ought to take it as a sign of grace that the man was valued at four times that of the horse.

Advertisements such as the above were common, as were also announcements, such as the following, of articles to be sold:—

"A very likely negro man aged 26. Two hundred thousand feet of seasoned lumber. Fifty acclimatized slaves, consisting of men, women and children. A number of hogsheads and jowls. A likely woman and her two children. Ten and a half barrels of mackerel. A likely negro, thirty-three years old. One hundred barrels of mess pork. Several likely negroes. Mrs. Gore's new novel, *The Birthright*. [61]

[60] Cited by Hart, *American History Told by Contemporaries*, ii., p. 300.

[61] Cited by J. R. Balme, *The American States, Churches, and the War*, p. 27.

The mixing of the goods was evidently designed to attract all classes of customers.

No useful end would be served by a mere multiplication of similar notices. Under Christian rule slaves were treated with a ferocity and lack of consideration that has never been surpassed and seldom equalled in the history of the world. They were bred as cattle are bred; husband and wife were separated and forced to mate again with as little compunction as cattle. They were herded like cattle, branded like cattle, sold like cattle. Legally the slave was not a *person* at all; he was a chattel; and domestically the matter was well stated by a clergyman—the Rev. R. Breckenridge:—

> In the eye of the law no coloured slave man is the husband of any wife in particular, nor any slave woman the wife of any husband in particular; no slave man is the father of any children in particular, and no slave child is the child of any parent in particular.[62]

But despite all the horror and degradation of Christian slavery, less than a hundred years ago, the Churches stood as its great bulwark, supplying a religious sanction and a moral justification. Thus, in 1836, the Charlestown Union Presbytery resolved—

> that in the opinion of this Presbytery, the holding of slaves, so far from being a SIN in the sight of God, is nowhere condemned in his holy word; that it is in accordance with the example, or consistent

[62] *Key to Uncle Tom's Cabin*, p. 406.

with the precepts of patriarchs, apostles, and prophets, and that it is compatible with the most fraternal regard to the best good of those servants whom God may have committed to our charge.[63]

When the picture of slavery as drawn by Mrs. Harriet Beecher Stowe was impugned, she replied by issuing *The Key to Uncle Tom's Cabin,* in which she cited all the facts upon which her story was based. The Harmony Presbytery of New Carolina resolved:—

> That whereas certain sundry persons in England and Scotland have denounced slavery as obnoxious to the laws of God. . . . Resolved, That slavery has existed from the days of those good old slaveholders and patriarchs, Abraham, Isaac, and Jacob (who are now in the kingdom of heaven) to the time when the apostle Paul sent a runaway slave home to his master Philemon, and wrote a Christian and fraternal letter to this slaveholder. . . . Resolved, that . . . the existence of slavery is not opposed to the will of God.[64]

The Charlestown Union Presbytery resolved:—

> That in the opinion of this Presbytery, the holding of slaves, so far from being a sin in the sight of God, is nowhere condemned in his holy word; that it is in accordance with the example, or consistent with the precepts of patriarchs, apostles, and prophets.[65]

The Georgia Annual Conference (Methodist) resolved

[63] *500,000 Strokes for Freedom,* Tract 8, p. 23.

[64] *Key to Uncle Tom's Cabin,* p. 384.

[65] *Ibid,* p. 384.

"it is the sense of the Georgia Annual Conference that slavery as it exists in the United States is not a moral evil."[66] At a public meeting composed of the clergy of Richmond, it was resolved "that the example of our Lord Jesus Christ and his apostles, in not interfering with the question of slavery . . . is worthy of the imitation of all ministers of the Gospel.[67] In the Northern Churches Mrs. Stowe records that, in 1836 the New York Presbytery decided that no one should be elected a deacon or an elder unless he gave a pledge that he would abstain from discussing the subject of slavery (p. 409). In Baltimore a somewhat similar resolution was passed. Generally, she sums up the situation by pointing out that the action of the Churches has been to *suppress* such anti-slavery feeling as existed some fifty years earlier. This, she says, is true of the Presbyterians. "Worse has been the history of the Methodist Church. The history of the Baptist Church shows the same principle; and as to the Episcopalian Church, it has never done anything *but* comply either with North or South" (p. 426). On this head Mrs. Stowe is quite borne out by Garrison.

What the clergy resolved on in General Assembly they loyally stood by in practice. The Rev. M. Peck said:—

If we go strongly against slavery we shall cast

[66] *Key to Uncle Tom's Cabin*, p. 386.

[67] *Ibid*, p. 399.

a gloom over the whole Christian Church. Let us leave the matter in the hands of God.[68]

Rev. James Wilson calls slavery:—

that gracious and benevolent system which elevates the heathen cannibal into the contented, civilized, intelligent, and happy domestics we see around us. Nay, more, into humble, faithful, and most joyous worshippers of the true and everlasting God. Bless God for such a system. We don't apologise for slavery, we glory in it, and no society shall exist within our borders that disqualifies or stigmatizes the slave trade.[69]

The attitude of the American Tract Society may be judged by the following, written by James Russell Lowell in 1858:—

If the pious men who founded the American Tract Society had been told that within forty years they would be watchful of their publications, lest, by inadvertence, anything disrespectful might be spoken of the African slave trade—that they would consider it an ample equivalent for compulsory dumbness on the vices of slavery, that their colporteurs could awaken the minds of Southern brethren to the horrors of St. Bartholomew—that they would hold their peace about the body of Cuffee dancing to the music of the cart-whip, provided only they could save the soul of Sambo alive by presenting him a pamphlet, which he could not read, on the depravity of the double shuffle—that they would be fellow-members

[68] *Report of Anti-Slavery Society.* New York. 1860.

[69] *Report of Anti-Slavery Society.* New York, 1860, p. 281.

> in the Tract Society with him who sold their fellow-members in Christ on the auction-block, if he agreed with them in condemning transubstantiation. . . . If these excellent men had been told this they would have shrunk in horror, and exclaimed: "Are thy servants dogs, that they should do these things?" Yet this is precisely the present position of the Society.

The Protestant Episcopal Society issued a pamphlet containing the formal declaration that "Without a new revelation from heaven no man was authorized to pronounce slavery wrong." Alexander Campbell, founder of the "Christian" sect, proclaimed the divine right of slavery. The Maine Universalists declined to express an opinion on the subject. A Cincinnati Conference (Methodist) declared itself "decidedly opposed to modern abolitionism, and asked its ministers to refrain from patronizing the Abolition movement." Wilbur Fiske, President of the Wesleyan University, Middleton, Conn., was described by Garrison as "an abusive and malignant opponent of Abolition." When, in 1845, the Northern Methodist Church showed signs of a better feeling, the immediate result was the secession of a number of churches and the formation of "The Methodist Episcopal Church, South." Fifteen years later (1860) when an attempt was made to induce the ministers of the Methodist Church to sign a protest against slavery, out of 14,000 ministers only 241 would append their names to the document.[70]

[70] *Report of Anti-Slavery Society*, N.Y., 1860, p. 282.

The Leeds (England) Anti-Slavery Society's report for 1860 contains a letter written by the Rev. H. Mattison, of New York, travelling preacher to the Northern Methodist Episcopal Church, in which he says: " I am fully satisfied from figures that we cannot have to-day less than 10,000 slaveholders, and 100,000 slaves in our Northern Methodist Episcopal Church, and the number is increasing every year. And, still worse, our people raise, and buy, and sell slaves as others do, without rebuke or hindrance." That this was no exaggeration is shown by the fact that at the Methodist Conference held at Buffalo in 1860, on one delegate suggesting a resolution against slavery, he was authoritatively informed that not ten delegates would support the resolution. It was just before this date that Garrison had written in the *Liberty Bell* that " in England and Scotland especially, extraordinary pains have been taken in public and in private to hold up the American Anti-Slavery Society as unworthy of all countenance in any degree, on account of its infidel character.[71]

The infidel character of Garrison's associates had already caused him trouble. One man had written him that he could not act with " Infidels like Fanny Wright and Abner Kneeland."[72] Garrison, when he visited

[71] Balme, *American States, Churches and the War*, p. 278.

[72] Fanny (Frances) Wright was a well known and extremely able Freethinking writer and speaker, born in Scotland, 1795. She was very early engaged in anti-slavery work. Abner Kneeland was born in 1774, founded the *Boston Investigator*, and was imprisoned for blasphemy.

Boston, found every church, chapel, and public meeting-place closed to him. It was, says his biographers, "left for a society of avowed 'infidels'" to offer him their hall. It was Abner Kneeland's society, its leader having only recently been imprisoned for blasphemy.

In the struggle against the Stuarts in the seventeenth century the bulwark of passive obedience and the divine right of kings was the New Testament. In America, two centuries later, the same documents were found useful against Abolitionists. Certainly the Young Men's American Bible Association was of that opinion, since it issued a specially annoted edition of the New Testament as an Anti-Abolitionist pamphlet.[73] The General Assembly of the Cumberland Presbyterian Church having seized a debtor's goods, and some negroes being among the effects, sold them and devoted the money *to missionary purposes.*[74] Shortly before this, at a meeting of the Baptist Missionary Union, one of the zealous brethren offered to sell one of his slaves for two hundred dollars if the buyer would send him to Africa to preach the Gospel among his coloured brethren. No one can question this slave-holding parson's zeal, nor doubt the touching story the slave-missionary would have to tell his people. No wonder the American Bible Society declined to interfere in the question of slavery. It numbered hundreds

[73] *New York Anti-Slavery Society Report,* 1860, p. 282.

[74] *Ibid,* p. 282.

of slaveholders among its published list of members. The influence of these pious slave-owners was indeed so powerful, that the well-known publishing firm of Harper Brothers issued an apology for having printed a work written by an Abolitionist.[75]

How could any of the Churches denounce slavery when so much of their money came from slave-owners? When did the Christian Churches denounce anything under such conditions? A Mississippi clergyman, the Rev. James Smylie, writing in defence of slavery, put the case in a nutshell:—

> If slavery be a sin, and if advertising and apprehending slaves with a view to returning them to their masters is a direct violation of the divine law, and if the buying, selling, or holding a slave for the sake of a gain is a heinous sin and scandal, then, verily, three-fourths of all the Episcopalians, Methodists, Baptists and Presbyterians, in eleven States of the Union are of the Devil. They hold, if they do not buy and sell slaves, and with few exceptions they hesitate not to apprehend and restore runaway slaves when in their power.[76]

Even after slavery had been officially destroyed in North America at the cost of a long and bitter war, the negro was still doomed to experience the true nature of Christian brotherhood. Slavery might be abolished, but the colour bar and the colour preju-

[75] *American Anti-Slavery Society's Report* for 1837, p. 376.

[76] *American Anti-Slavery Society's Report* for 1837, p. 386.

dice, substantially unknown, as we have seen, to the Pagan world, remained. Laws that hold good for the white man do not hold good for the black. Even when the law fails to discriminate, public opinion does. An able and unquestionable authority on the condition of the negro in the United States, Dr. W. E. B. Du Bois, writing in 1911, thus sums up the situation.[77] In the Southern States negroes cannot vote, or their votes are neutralized by fraud; they live in the least desirable districts and receive low wages; they cannot by law marry whites; they cannot join white churches or attend white colleges, white hotels or places of public entertainment; receive a distinct standard of justice in the courts, and are exposed to mob law; are taxed for parks and public libraries which they may not enter; are often unable to protect their homes from invasion and their savings from exploitation. In the North, legal disabilities do not exist, but the negro is often refused accommodation at hotels, etc., and is made to feel himself an undesirable.

Very much more might be said on the question of Christianity and slavery, but in the nature of the case it could only be a repetition in kind of what has already been said. And, truly, the case against Christianity is plain and damning. Never, during the whole of its history has it spoken in a clear voice against slavery;

[77] *Inter-Racial Problems*, p. 361.

always, as we have seen, its chief supporters have been pronounced believers. They have cited religious teaching in its defence, they have used all the power of the Churches for its maintenance. Naturally, in a world in which the vast majority are professing Christians, believers are to be found on the side of humanity and justice. But to that the reply is plain. Men are human before they are Christian; both history and experience point to the constant lesson of the many cases in which the claims of a developing humanity override those of an inculcated religious teaching.

But the damning fact against Christianity is, not that it found slavery here when it arrived, and accepted it as a settled institution, not even that it is plainly taught in its "sacred" books, but that it deliberately created a new form of slavery, and for hundreds of years invested it with a brutality greater than that which existed centuries before. A religion which could tolerate this slavery, argue for it, and fight for it, cannot by any stretch of reasoning be credited with an influence in forwarding emancipation. Christianity no more abolished slavery than it abolished witchcraft, the belief in demonism, or punishment for heresy. It was the growing moral and social sense of mankind that compelled Christians and Christianity to give up these and other things.[78]

[78] Most of us, I think, are apt to forget at what recent date Christian countries gave up the practice of owning slaves.

As a system, Christianity was irrevocably committed to the institution of slavery. That modern Christians try to prove otherwise may be taken as only one more instance of the disintegrating effect of new ideas and new institutions on old customs and beliefs.

The first European country to abolish slavery was revolutionary France, 1791. This was afterwards reintroduced, and finally abolished in 1848. Denmark abolished slavery in 1792; Spain, 1820; Sweden, 1814; Holland, 1863; Portugal, 1878; England, 1833; United States, 1865-8. Modified forms lingered on in some places, and the improvements were sometimes more a matter of form than of fact. The exploitation of the coloured people on the Congo and elsewhere in our own day, I pass for the moment, although very much might be said of the horrors and injustice of this practical enslavement of coloured labour.

VI.

Christianity and Labour

◆ ◆

On the ground of historic fact there is, as we have seen, not the slightest justification for the plea that Christianity destroyed the institution of slavery. No one is able to show when or where the Churches authoritatively condemned slavery; and, on the other hand, there is the evidence, derived from Christian countries in all parts of the world, that slavery found its most ardent supporters in the most orthodox circles, and that, in the upholding of slavery, the Old and New Testaments were relied upon for support. The evidence is clear and final. It certainly could not be for lack of power that the Christian Church did not condemn slavery. For many centuries it exercised a position of commanding influence. It claimed the power to make and unmake kings, whole nations trembled at the threat of excommunication; it could set nation fighting nation for a difference of religious belief; it could send the whole of Europe on such a madman's errand as the Crusades; it could burn and imprison hundreds of thousands for witchcraft and heresy. The Church lacked neither power nor opportunity. And yet, it not only failed to destroy slavery; under its auspices there was impressed upon the world the most brutal and degraded slave system known to man.

Beaten off the ground of historic fact, the plea is put forward that by bringing into the world a new respect for labour, a new love and care for the hitherto despised "lower classes," by humanising the relations between human beings, the influence of Christianity made for the destruction of slavery by elevating the tone of human society. This plea is quite modern, it was seldom made during the time that slavery existed as an established institution, and is only one of the means by which Christian controversialists seek to meet and repel the Freethought attack. And to that one may well reply by asking the value of an influence that takes the larger part of two thousand years to make itself felt, which is weakest when Christianity is strongest, and strongest when the rejection of Christianity by educated men and women is a familiar phenomenon all over the civilised world.

The claim is wholly false. In its earliest manifestation, Christianity aimed at supernatural salvation, not at secular reform. To say that it preached to the "poor and lowly" is beside the point. That is the lot of most religious movements struggling for recognition, and Christianity limited its preaching to the poor only while it had no other audience. When its position changed it became a preaching *to* the poor in defence of the privileges and possessions of the rich. Moreover, so soon as we find ourselves in contact with Christianity as an historic fact, it is the figure of the monk, not the social reformer, that dominates the stage. We see Christianity eating its way into the vitals of the Roman Empire, and we see social institutions and civil life withering before its advance.

So far as Christianity is concerned, the labouring classes remain "hewers of wood and drawers of water." Their fortune lay between having a good owner or a bad one. Here the bishop might have treated them more liberally than the baron, there the baron read the bishop a lesson in humanity. But it is safe to say that, under mediæval Christian rule, labour was held in greater contempt than under Pagan Rome. For centuries the working classes pass almost unnoticed by writers and historians. What Professor Thorold Rogers says of the seventeenth century: "There are no annals of these people, of their work, and of their sufferings. . . . History, which crowds its canvas with these great names, tells us nothing of the people," may truthfully be said of the preceding centuries. This, we may be sure, was not because there was no opposition, no poverty, no social wrong. It was simply that the labouring class had not "emerged."

During the mediæval period the heads of the Church exercised all the rights of a feudal lord, and were even more tenacious of their privileges. The serf was disabled from migrating from one part of the country to another. His daughter could not marry without the consent of the lord, who frequently demanded payment for permission; or, worse still, the infamous "Right of the first night." The serf was tied down in a hundred and one ways, and it is highly significant of the esteem in which the Church was held, that in every peasant revolt that occurred there was always a direct attack on the Church.

Writing about the twelfth century, Professor Thorold Rogers says of the homes of the poorer classes:—

> The houses of these villagers were mean and dirty. Brickmaking was a lost art, stone was found only in a few places. . . . The wood fire was on a hob of clay. Chimneys were unknown, except in castles and manor houses, and the smoke escaped through the door or whatever other aperture it could reach. . . . The floor of the homestead was filthy enough, but the surroundings were filthier still. Close by the door stood the mixen, a collection of every abomination—streams from which, in rainy weather, fertilised the lower meadows, generally the lord's special pasture, and polluted the stream. . . . The house of the peasant cottager was poorer still. Most of them were probably built of posts wattled

and plastered with clay or mud, with an upper storey of poles reached by a ladder.[79]

What the lord took he held by right of force; what the Church had it held by force of cunning. And as, in the long run, the cunning of the Church was more powerful than the force of the robber-lord, the priesthood grew in riches until its wealth became a threat to the whole of the community. In England in the thirteenth century the clergy numbered one in fifty-two of the population, and the possessions of the Church included a third of the land of England. No opportunity was lost by the Church to drain money from the people whether they were rich or poor. The trade done in candles, and sales of indulgences brought in large sums of money, and there were continuous disputes between the clergy and the king and the Pope as to the divisions of the spoil.

There is a curious illustration of this in the case of Thomas à Becket. Becket was killed in mid-winter, and directly after his death the miracles that occurred at the tomb of Becket brought money into the coffers of the Church. But mid-winter was not a good time for pilgrimages, and so the monks sought permission of the Pope, Honorius the third, to change the day of "translation" from mid-winter to mid-summer. The Pope was agreeable but claimed half the gross profits of the shrine. The monks protested that this

[79] *Six Centuries of Work and Wages*, p. 67.

would not leave them enough to carry on their business, and in the end the Pope consented to take half the net profits.

Mr. G. G. Coulton, writing of the fifteenth century, says :—

> The great church and its steeple dominated the whole landscape; under that church, as the villager well knew, very few monks were content with anything like his own sparing fare, while others were able to entertain the baron, or even the king, on equal terms. The cellarer or the granger, when they came into the fields, looked down from their palfreys upon the labourers; and the friendliest talk was, frankly and necessarily, condescending; the bailiff, again, so rigorous to his inferiors, was on his best manners before the monastic official. The doles and broken meats distributed at the almonry were, as everybody knew, produced not by the monks, but by the peasant's toil; and often they amounted to far less than the tithes which the monks drew, in that very parish, from the peasant's own sheaves, Or again, if the monastery were too far distant for its actual walls to be seen, still there came this occasional monastic "outrider" to collect his dues or to screw up the labourer to his work; while often in the fifteenth century, worse still, the monk was scarcely seen at all, but known mainly as an absentee landlord who had farmed out the estates to some enterprising middleman.[80]

The picture of the Church watching over the poor,

[80] *Five Centuries of Religion,* Vol. II, p. 16.

sheltering them from wrong, tending them in sickness, and relieving them in their poverty will not do. It is totally without historic foundation. When the poor revolted, and apart from the great revolts, there were many small and local outbreaks, the anger of the poor was directed as much against the Church as it was against the nobles. Some Churchmen were good men, but that is true of laymen at all times and in all countries. The Church did attend the sick, but its trade was in miracle cures and prayers, and so they very much resembled men hawking their own goods and attending to their own business. And there is the plain, historic fact, that in defence of its miracle cures it did what it could to obstruct the growth of both medical and sanitary science.[81] It did give alms, but these constituted but a small part of what it had previously taken.

The poor man was substantially the property of someone, and whether that someone happened to be the Church or a secular lord made very little difference. The Bishop claimed all the rights of the feudal lord, but he managed to rid himself of most of their obligations. Few of the ordinary duties that fell upon the layman fell upon the cleric. They repudiated the ordinary processes of law, claiming that the Church was above ordinary secular claims, they also possessed

[81] See White's *Warfare Between Science and Theology,* Vol. II.

the right of taxing themselves independently of the rest of the community.[82] Much of the land acquired by the Churches was given to them as guarantees for the community,[83] and in the case of tithe, part of it was to be set aside for charity. The Church, however, ignored most obligations in these directions.

To talk of the Church as the friend of the poor is idle. The Church naturally protected its own slaves or serfs against the assaults of other owners; but that differed in no respect from the way in which one noble resisted the assault of other nobles. Property may be always depended upon to safeguard itself. But when one applies such a test case as the Statute of Labourers, one finds it receiving the full support of the Church until it was repealed in the time of Elizabeth.[84] And of the general attitude of the ruling classes, Professor Rogers says: "I contend that from 1563 to 1824, a conspiracy concocted by the law and carried out by the parties interested in its success, was entered into, to cheat the English workman of his

[82] P. V. Smith, *History of English Institutions*, p. 15.

[83] See *History of the Law of Real Property*, by K. E Digby, ch.

[84] By this statute no person under sixty years of age, whether serf or freeman, could decline to take wages as paid in 1347. The lord had the first claim to the labour of his serfs, and any who declined to work were to be imprisoned. Anyone found paying more than the fixed wages could be fined. Alms were forbidden to all able-bodied labourers. Any excess of wages paid or received could be seized by the king.

wages, to tie him to the soil, to deprive him of hope, and to degrade him into irremediable poverty."[84A] That was the net result of the influence of Christianity, and of the activity of the Christian Church in spreading abroad a spirit of kindliness, humanity and brotherhood!

The conduct of the Church, as a matter of fact, differed in hardly any respect, save for a preaching to the poor, and a repetition of gospel platitudes about the blessings of poverty, and the duty of charity, from that of the secular landowner or capitalist. It claimed all their privileges and exacted from those under them every due, and in extracting these dues it had the additional force of spiritual terrorism and spiritual punishment.

I might cite a very large number of authorities to prove these statements; it will save space and time if I summarise a very compact and authoritative statement of the case as given in the fourth and fifth chapters of the second volume of G. G. Coulton's "Five Centuries of Religion," a work which while primarily aiming at disproving certain Roman Catholic claims, serves as a not less devastating criticism of Christian claims as a whole.

Citing contemporary and official records he shows how monk, abbot and bishop lorded it over the peasant with an even more rigorous rule than the tem-

[84a] *Six Centuries,* p. 398.

poral lord. For the latter might at times give free rein to his more generous impulses and remit claims or grant freedom. But the abbot or bishop was tied down by the rules of the Church and forbidden, in the name of the Church, to anything that would weaken either its power or its wealth.

The extensive remains of the old monasteries, and other religious buildings, are alone evidence of their wealth and power. Vale Royal in Cheshire, was built for one hundred monks at the cost of about (in modern values) three-quarters of a million sterling. In 1509 these buildings were occupied by nineteen monks. It should also be stated that by this time about half of the buildings were given up to public purposes. At Bury there were in 1280, 111 servants to eighty monks. At Ramsay, Evesham, Meaux, and elsewhere the proportion of servants to monks was equally remarkable. It is calculated that at the Dissolution the workmen and servants attached to these religious houses outnumbered the monks. In addition to these servants directly attached to the religious houses there were the serfs and tenants who came under the heading of freemen. Against all these the Church exacted the mediæval dues and rights. The children of the serf was the property of the lord, and where a serf belonging to one lord was permitted to marry a serf belonging to another lord, the children of the marriage were equally divided. Coulton notes that in documents dealing with the serf the word family was seldom used, the children came under the head of "brood," or *sequela*. Neither male nor female serf was permitted to marry without the consent of their lord, lay or religious. There was also the right of "Heriot," in virtue of which the lord claimed a death duty amounting to about half of the possessions of the widow, and her orphans, and, says Coulton, "this was exacted as pitilessly by the monk as by the layman; here and there a saint might remit it, but of no monastery do we read what is to be found in a lay lord's charter of about 1200, in which Richard de Flete, at the prayers of his wife and for the sake of his own and his kinsfolk's souls, solemnly abandons from henceforth his right of taking from the widow and her orphan children a death duty."

In every respect the Church—the daring and spontaneous action of a good man here who risked both civil displeasure and spiritual displeasure excepted—was committed to stand definitely on the side of the mediæval ruler. He supported the order and sanctified it, and there is small wonder that whenever a distracted peasantry was roused to revolt, the revolt was as much against the priest as it was against the secular noble. Any claim for the creation of either legal rights or remissions of dues went equally against monk and lord. These were the two pillars of the existing system. They hung together; it was the only way they could resist being hung separately. The position is thus summarised by Coulton :—

> There is no doubt that, on the whole, the church was definitely on the lord's side. . . . Wycliffe is, I believe, the only mediaeval philosopher who expressly refuses to justify serfdom in theory. It has been asserted . . . that the gradual mitigation and the final extinction of servitude was mainly due to the church, and especially to the monks. . . . No evidence has ever been produced apart from one or two hints from the very earliest days of doubtful legends, for monks doing what lay lords and ladies fairly often did, that is, freeing considerable numbers of serfs, without payment, for the good of the owner's soul, for nearly all the monastic enfranchisements recorded, we have either explicit documentary evidence that the serf bought his liberty with hard cash, or have strong reason to suspect it. . . . It is often complained of spendthrift abbots or officials that they are embezzling conventual property by granting manumissions and pocketing the money. For if a Churchman was of all men the most unwilling manumitter, this was partly because the thing was forbidden both in conscience and in law. . . . Canon law explicitly forbade alienation of serfs as of any other kind of property; and English records show how, in the few cases where a bishop wanted to free a trusty servant who was not too decrepit to have lost his market value, he found it advisable to secure himself by procuring papal license. Serfdom, therefore, lasted longest of all on ecclesiastical, and specially monastic, estates; there were about 30,000 in France

when the Revolution broke out. . . . The peasant, then, knew the monk mainly as a lord not very different from other lords. Alms were given at the Abbey gate, but far less than is commonly supposed; and if these had been multiplied fourfold, they would not have equalled what the monks drew from their rights, hallowed by custom and law, of taking to their own use the greater part of the endowments of a large number of parishes.

Through all the changes of the sixteenth, seventeenth, and eighteenth centuries it is impossible to detect anxiety on the part of the Churches, Roman Catholic or Protestant, to better the status or improve the condition of the working classes. Whatever improvements may have come about—and they were few enough—came independently of Christianity, organised or unorganised. Controversies about religious matters might, and did, grow more acute; controversies about bettering the position of the working classes only began with the breaking down of Christianity. And when, as in Germany, there occurred a peasants' revolt,[85] and the peasants appealed to Luther for assistance, he wrote, after exhorting the peasants to resignation, to the nobles :—

A rebel is outlawed of God and Kaiser, therefore

[85] The objects of the revolt (1525) were stated in twelve articles. These demanded that the community should appoint its own ministers, that only authorized persons should collect tithes, an alteration of the game laws, mitigation of feudal service, restoration of communal lands, etc., with an offer to reconsider any provision that might later be found to be unjust.

> who can and will first slaughter such a man does right well, since upon such a common rebel every man is alike judge and executioner. Therefore, who can shall here openly or secretly smite, slaughter and stab, and hold that there is nothing more poisonous, more harmful, more devilish than a rebellious man.[86]

In England the "reformed" Churches were concerned, not with a bettering of the working-class, but with the gathering of wealth and power into their hands. And in pre-revolutionary France the Church saw unmoved a state of affairs almost unimaginable, so far as the masses of the people were concerned, in their misery and demoralisation. At a time when half the land of France, in addition to palaces, chateaux, and other forms of wealth was possessed by the nobility and clergy, and were practically free from taxation, a contemporary writes:—

> Certain savage-looking beings, male and female, are seen in the country, black, livid, and sunburnt, and belonging to the soil which they dig and grub with invincible stubbornness. They seem capable of articulation, and when they stand erect they display human lineaments. They are, in fact, men. They retire at night into their dens, where they live on black bread, water, and roots. They spare other human beings the trouble of sowing.[87]

[86] Cited by Karl Pearson, *Ethics of Freethought*, p. 226.

[87] Van Laun, *The French Revolutionary Epoch*, Vol. I., p. 23.

In pre-revolutionary France the clergy, counting monks and nuns, numbered, in 1762, over four hundred thousand, with total possessions estimated at two thousand million pounds, producing an annual revenue of about one hundred and forty millions. The clergy were free from taxation, and the higher members of the order possessed all the rights and privileges of the feudal nobility. To the end the Church in France—as in our day in pre-revolutionary Russia—remained the champion of privilege and misgovernment. "The feudal Church," says Mr. W. M. Sloane, "was the cement of French society to a higher degree than the absolute monarchy."[88]

As a final test of the influence of Christianity we may take a rapid survey of the attitude of the Churches during the formative period of the English working-class movement.

The closing years of the eighteenth century and the first thirty years of the nineteenth saw the organisation of the English manufacturing system. It was marked by the rise of a wealthy manufacturing class—made wealthy by cotton, iron, and coal—by the creation of a huge proletariat, landless, miserably poor, working under conditions of almost unbelievable degradation, and hampered by ferocious laws which deliberately aimed at the enslavement of a whole class.

[88] *The French Revolution and Religious Reform.* Introduction, xxiii.

During this period the finishing touches were given to the process of driving the people off the land and into the factories. The "English Factory System" was established, and if ever there has existed in the history of the world, and in a civilised country a more brutal system than that, the present writer has yet to meet it.

Let us take a bird's-eye view of the conditions of labour during this period. To begin with, woman and child labour was common in both mines and factories. Child labour was drawn from two classes. There were what was called "free-labour children," that is, children living at home with their parents, and apprentice children, those that were apprenticed to the masters by the different parishes. These children were apprenticed until they were twenty-one years, commencing usually when they were seven years of age; but Robert Owen asserts that children as young as five were taken. The regular working hours were from 5 a.m. till 8 p.m., with six full days' labour per week. Their bed consisted of a dirty blanket to sleep on and another for covering. In the case of the parish children, a regular traffic was built up between Lancashire and other parts of England, and, says Mr. and Mrs. Hammond, in one case at least, a Lancashire mill-owner agreed to take one idiot with every twenty children.[89] The mortality was high, the cruelty

[89] Cited in *The Town Labourer*, p. 145.

even under the kindest masters, could not but be great.

Sir Samuel Romily says :—

It is a very common practice with the great populous parishes in London to bind children in large numbers to the proprietors of cotton-mills in Lancashire and Yorkshire, at a distance of 200 miles. The children who are sent off by waggon loads at a time, are as much lost for ever to their parents as if they were shipped off for the West Indies. The parishes that bind them, by procuring a settlement for the children at the end of forty days, get rid of them for ever; and the poor children have not a human being in the world to whom they can look up for redress against the wrongs they may be exposed to from these wholesale dealers in them, whose object it is to get everything they can possibly wring from their excessive labour and fatigue.[89A]

The mills were hotbeds of what was called "putrid fever," but it is pleasing to record that, despite the fact of children working fifteen and sixteen hours a day under the most unhealthy conditions, in spite, too, of their being poorly fed and clothed, their religious education was not neglected. The Christian conscience of the British public would never have tolerated that. And, in one case, when the conduct of some mill-owners at Backbarrow was impugned, they promptly produced the following from two clergymen :—

We, the undersigned, do hereby certify, that we

[89a] *Life, By Himself,* Vol. II., p. 188.

attend every Sabbath-day at the apprentice house of Ainsworth, Catterall & Company and accompany the children to Finsthwaite Chapel for the morning's service; that in the afternoon we teach them to read in the Bible, New Testament, or Spelling Book, according to their ability, and that every attention is paid to the strict observance of the Sabbath.

J. Slater.

William Fernix.[90]

In the mines the conditions were, if possible, still worse. In 1842, there was presented to both Houses of Parliament a Report from the Children's Employment Commissioners. From a summary of this report, published in the *Westminster Review* for October, 1842, and extending over fifty pages, I take the following. Of the extent of child labour in mines, we are told :—

Children are taken at the earliest ages, if only to be used as living and waving candlesticks, or to keep rats from a dinner; and it is in pits of this worst character, too, in which most female children are employed. It would appear from the practical returns obtained by the Commissioner, that about one-third of the persons employed in coal mines are under eighteen years of age, and that much more than one-third of this proportion are under thirteen years of age.

In Shropshire we learn " there are *very few under six or seven* who are employed to draw weights with

[90] Cited in *The Town Labourer*, p. 148.

a girdle round the body; and those only when the roof of the pit is so low for short distances as to prevent horses of the smallest size from being employed." Of a Yorkshire pit, in describing the way the children draw the trucks of coal—from two to five cwt., "they buckle round their naked person a broad leather strap, to which is attached in front a broad ring and about four feet of chain, terminating in a hook." No wonder the Commissioners speak of these human beasts of burden, chained, fettered, and harnessed, as "presenting an appearance indescribably disgusting and unnatural."

In the West Riding there was no distinction of sex so far as underground labour was concerned. "The men work in a state of perfect nakedness, and are in this state assisted in their labours by females of all ages, from girls of six years old up to women of twenty-one, these females being quite naked down to the waist." Pages might be filled with similar descriptions of pits in England, Scotland and Wales. The whole forms a striking comment on Canon Brownlow's statement that "One of the most remarkable effects of Christianity was . . . the rehabilitation of manual labour in public estimation."[91]

One ought to say a word or two on the employment of boys in sweeping chimneys—a practice unknown outside the British Isles—before leaving this aspect of

[91] *Slavery and Serfdom*, p. 47.

the subject. Children of six or seven were employed at this task, although an Act was passed in 1817 ordering that no boy should be employed under eight years of age. Most of these boys were either sold outright to the employers by callous parents, or apprenticed from the parish. They were set to climbing chimneys, and often straw was lit behind them to encourage quickness of movement. Some masters washed their boys once a week, others just left them alone. The boys were stunted in growth, blear-eyed from the soot, and "flapper-kneed" from climbing. Deaths from suffocation were common. Yet, when in 1803, a very mild Bill was brought before the House of Lords, regulating the trade, it was rejected by a House consisting of one Archbishop, five Bishops, three Dukes, five Earls, one Viscount, and ten Barons.

It only remains to add that during the existence of these complicated horrors, and the systematic ill-treatment and slaughter of children for pure gain, the country was bristling with renewed religious activities, imprisoning men and women for publishing and selling Paine's *Age of Reason*, and fighting France in *defence of civilisation*.

It is only necessary to add here, with regard to adult male labour, the savagery with which attempts made by working men to improve the conditions of employment were punished by the law, and without a single one of the Churches raising a protest. Men were imprisoned, fined, and transported under the operation of the Combination Laws. Protests came from Freethinkers like Place, Robert Owen, Carlile, Cobbett, Lovett, and others; leading Christians remained silent, as did also the Churches. Indeed, Wilberforce, noted for his piety and his exertions on behalf of the negro, was one of the chief defenders of the Combination Laws which, for over a quarter of a century, meant the practical enslavement of the working classes. It was the Christian method of bringing about "a rehabilitation of manual labour in public estimation."[92]

One other matter, and then we can pass to the part played by Christianity during this period. Churches were plentiful, and religious activity, as we shall see later, was great. But education was at the lowest ebb. The report of the Commissioners already cited stated that in none of the towns which had sprung up in connection with mining or manufactures was there any provision made for education. In Derbyshire, colliers'

[92] It is also worth noting that the practice of building soldiers' barracks all over England dates from this period. This was not a military measure, but a measure of police. The practice had been to quarter the soldiers with the people. But when unrest arose among the working classes, it was pointed out in a Home Office Report that unless soldiers could be kept away from the people, they could not be depended on in an emergency. It was this report that led to the building of barracks in all the manufacturing districts. The real motive was openly admitted by Pitt in the House of Commons (see *The Town Labourer*, pp. 83-4.)

children were excluded by rule from the few schools that existed. In Oldham and Ashton, with a population of 105,000, there was not a single public day school for poor children. In Lancashire and Cheshire, forty per cent. of the men and sixty-five per cent. of the women getting married could not sign their names.[93] And yet, when the Education Bill of 1819 came before the House of Lords, out of eighteen Bishops who voted on the measure, fifteen voted against it. They, as Mr. and Mrs. Hammond say, "objected to any system that put the control of education out of the hands of the bishop of the diocese." The real impulse to educating the poor came largely from Robert Owen, the man who declared that "all the religions of the world were so many forms of geographical insanity."

There was, indeed, a deeply rooted objection to education on the part of the governing world, secular and religious. One speaker put it bluntly in the House of Commons:—

> However specious in theory the project might be, of giving education to the labouring classes of the poor, it would in effect be found to be prejudicial to their morals and happiness; it would teach them to despise their lot in life instead of making them good servants in agriculture, and other laborious employments in which their rank in society had destined them, instead of teaching them subordina-

[93] *The Town Labourer*, p. 55.

tion, it would render them factious and refractory, as was evident in the manufacturing counties; it would enable them to read seditious pamphlets, seditious books, and publications against Christianity.[94]

But if oppression was rife, education at a low ebb, and misery prevalent,[95] the religion of the people was receiving attention. The period was, in fact, one of revival in religion. The Wesleyan revival was in full swing, and evangelical Christianity was making great advances. Between 1799 and 1804 there were founded The British and Foreign Bible Society, The London Missionary Society, The Religious Tract Society, The Church Missionary Society, The Christian Knowledge Society, and The Mission to the Jews. Quite a number of smaller societies came into existence during this period.

Parliament, which looked with composure at the position of the working-classes, voted one million two hundred thousand sterling for Church building[96] in 1820, and a further half million in 1824. Between 1801

[94] Cited by Mr. and Mrs. Hammond, p. 57

[95] In 1839, in Liverpool, there were 7,860 cellars used as dwellings by 39,000 people—one seventh of the population. Out of 37,000 habitations examined, 18,400 were ill-furnished and 10,400 altogether without furniture. In Bury, out of 3,000 families visited 773 slept three and four in a bed, 209 four or five in a bed, in sixty-seven six slept altogether in a bed. Many other towns furnished similar examples.—(*Life of Robert Owen*, by Lloyd Jones, Vol. II., pp. 15-17).

[96] *Annual Report on Church Building*. Parl. Papers, Vol. V., Session, 1820. At that time one Englishman out of every seven was a pauper.

and 1831 no less than 500 new Churches were built. Between 1809 and 1829, £1,000,000 was granted to augment the salaries of the poorer clergy.

At this date the Archbishops of York and Canterbury were taking between them £52,930 annually; twenty-four bishops received £244,185; twenty-eight deans, £44,250; and 601 archdeacons, chancellors, prebendaries, and canons, £337,900 (see *The Extraordinary Black Book*, 1831, p. 54). At present the two Archbishops have to struggle along with only £24,000, while twenty-seven bishops must make ends meet on no more than £134,300. Nearly £3,000,000 of the Churches' income is derived from tithe, which was originally granted on condition that one-fourth should be returned to the poor. About £300,000 comes from Mining Royalties, of which about £240,000 comes from the county of Durham.

It would be unfair not to point out that England's "pastors and masters" were, during this period, as keen in suppressing Freethinking as they were in promoting Christianity. The influence of such men as Bentham, Shelley, Paine, Owen, Hardy, Thelwall, Place, Cobbett, Bamford, Prentice, Detrossier, Doherty, Hetherington, Carlile, Lovett, Godwin, and others, was felt and dreaded. In England and Scotland, men and women were imprisoned for selling or discussing Paine's writings. Carlile spent over nine years in prison for this offence, and Mr. and Mrs.

Hammond relate an amusing case in this connection. In 1819 a man was arrested for selling Paine's works. He was thrown into prison, and remained there until some "respectable gentleman" wrote to the Home Office pointing out that a mistake had been made. The pamphlet was written *against* Paine, and the agent was a good Christian. The pamphlet was a vile production, composed by Mrs. Trimmer, of the Religious Tract Society. The man was at once released. But it was probably the one case in connection with the Paine prosecution that deserved severe treatment.

So far, we have seen, side by side with the bringing to a head of that conspiracy to enslave the English working classes, referred to by Professor Thorold Rogers, a great development of religious activity. And the two things are really closely connected. Just as in the earlier centuries, and contemporaneously in America, Christianity was used as a means of keeping chattel-slaves docile and contented with their servitude; so, during the rise of the modern labour movement, it was used as an instrument to control the working classes and to prevent reforms. The governing classes were content with the employment of women and girls, almost nude, in mines; they viewed unmoved the horrors of child labour and all the evils of the factory system; little protest was raised against the criminal laws, which then punished over two hundred offences with death, but they were alive to the necessity of keeping the people religious. Parliament could vote huge sums of money for the building of churches, and at the same time reconcile itself to thousands of families living in cellars and lacking the bare decencies of life. This after centuries of a religion which had enjoyed greater wealth and power for a longer period than has ever fallen to any other creed.

Mr. and Mrs. Hammond, in the work from which I have already cited, also give one of the most damning indictments of Christianity and of the period with which I am acquainted, with examples from people of such unimpeachable Christian conviction as Hannah More and William Wilberforce.

Hannah More was, in the accepted sense of the term, a "good woman." She was certainly kindly natured and benevolent. She writes of villages in which "there is not one creature that can give a cup of broth to save a life"; of another in which a poor woman was condemned to death for attempting to steal butter that was offered at an unreasonable price; of girls taken into the coal pits at nine years of age. And yet, as Mr. and Mrs. Hammond say, it never appears to have crossed her mind that "it was desirable that men and women should have decent wages, or decent homes, or that there was something wrong with the arrangements of a society that left the mass of people in this plight." Instead, we find her writing to the people of Shipham, in 1801, during a time of scarcity :—

> Let me remind you that probably the very scarcity has been permitted by an all-wise and gracious Providence to unite all ranks of society together, to show the poor how immediately they are dependent upon the rich; and to show both rich and poor that they are dependent upon Himself.

Wilberforce, who took an active part in the creation of the Combination Laws of 1799-1800, which made it a criminal offence for half-a-dozen men to join together to secure a rise in wages or an improvement in the conditions of labour, wrote, in his *Practical View of the System of Christianity,* which he described as "the basis of all politics," that religion taught the poor to be diligent, humble, and patient, and advises them—

> that their more lowly path has been allotted them by the hand of God; that it is their part faithfully to discharge its duties and contentedly to bear its inconveniences. . . . Having food and raiment they should be content . . . that all human distinctions will soon be done away with, and the true followers of Christ will all, as children of the same Father, be alike admitted to the possession of the same heavenly inheritance.

When, during the suspension of the Habeas Corpus, Burdett pointed to the number of persons thrown into prison without trial, kept in solitary confinement, and forbidden communication with the outside world, he asked Wilberforce what a Christian was to think of those who not only did not visit the prisoner themselves, but would not allow others to visit him? Wilberforce replied that, "Religion had taught him to value the blessings the country enjoyed, and to hand them down to posterity unimpaired."

Every attempt to improve the condition of the working classes became identified with an attack on Christianity. Moreover, the French Revolution, with its stirring demand of "Liberty, Equality, and Fraternity," had thoroughly frightened the English governing classes. It was then, as in the 1914-18 War, a fight for ideals, and the ideal of Christian England was lower than that of Freethinking France. Says Mr. and Mrs. Hammond:—

> At the time when half Europe was intoxicated, and the other half maddened by the new magic of the word citizen, the English nation was in the hands of men who regarded the idea of citizenship as a challenge to their religion and their civilisation; who deliberately sought to make the inequalities of life the basis of the State, and to emphasise and perpetuate the position of the workpeople as a subject class. Hence it happened that the French Revolution has divided the people of France less than the Industrial Revolution has divided the people of England. For behind all the catastrophes and convulsions that seemed to the English upper classes the scum of the French Revolution, there was a constant and living inspiration, the sense of citizen-

ship; whereas the Industrial Revolution, that seemed to represent peaceful and constructive progress, inspired the separatist notion that the mass of men, women and children were not the citizens of to-day or the citizens of to-morrow, but merely part of the machinery that the great industry plied and handled.[97]

That was the way in which Christianity brought about the "rehabilitation of manual labour in public estimation." "The poor ye have always with you," said Jesus, and the poor, overworked, underfed, badly housed, and uneducated, were told to be content, to be grateful for the mercies shown them, and to look for their reward in the world to come.

Writing in the *Political Register* of January 3rd, 1824, Cobbett said of the Methodists:—

> The bitterest foes in England have been, and are, the Methodists. . . . The friends of freedom have found fault, and justly found fault, with the main body of the established clergy . . . but, hostile to freedom as the established clergy have been, their hostility has been nothing in point of virulence compared with that of these ruffian sectaries. . . . Books upon books they write. Tracts upon tracts. Villainous sermons upon villainous sermons they preach. Rail they do like Cropper and Bott Smith against the West Indian shareholders; but not a word do you ever hear from them against the shareholders in Lancashire or Ireland. On the contrary, they are continually telling the people here that they ought to

[97] *The Town Labourer*, pp. 325-6.

thank the Lord for the blessings they enjoy; that they ought to thank the Lord, not for a bellyful and a warm back, but for that abundant grace of which they are the bearers, and for which they charge them only one penny per week each.

It is certain that in this respect the working class leaders agreed in the main with Cobbett's view of the influence of the Methodist movement. Whatever good it did to the working class movement was incidental. What it aimed at was what primitive Christianity aimed at, inducing contentment with misery and injustice in this world in order to reap salvation hereafter. In less violent language, Mr. and Mrs. Hammond say the same as Cobbett:—

> If we look into the life and teaching of this new religion we can see that the whole spirit of its mission was unfavourable to the democratic movement and the growth of the Trade Union spirit. The Methodist movement was a call, not for citizens, but for saints; not for the vigorous, still less for the violent redress of injustice, but for the ecstatic vision, the perfect peace of expectation. The brutal inequalities of life, the wrongs inflicted on man by man, the hardships of poverty and suffering, these vexations of a passing world were merely trials of faith for the true Christian, who could escape from them and sustain his soul with dreams of a noble and confidential companionship in this world and of radiant happiness hereafter. The reform that he wanted had nothing to do with Parliament or Corn Laws or Combination Laws. In so far as this

religion touched on the affairs of this world it tended to reflect the spirit of its first missionary. It taught patience where the Trade Unions taught impatience. The Trade Union movement taught that men and women should use their power to destroy the supremacy of wealth in a world made by man; the Methodist that they should learn resignation amid the painful chaos of a world so made, for good reasons of his own, by God. . . . It set up a rival to the ideal of civic freedom. It diverted energy from the class struggle at a time when wise energy was scarce, and money when money was still scarcer. It would be extremely interesting to know what money was spent on religion by a class that was thereby diverting its resources from a war for independence. . . . The teaching of Methodism was unfavourable to working-class movements; its leaders were hostile, and its ideals, perhaps, increasingly hostile.

In their latest work, "The Age of the Chartists," the same authors give further and detailed proof of what has just been said. They point out that the leaders of the Radical and Reform movements were men such as Place, Lovatt, Carlile, Hetherington, Holyoake, Watson, Cooper, etc., all of whom were widely known for their anti-Christian opinions, and some of whom had actually served terms of imprisonment for blasphemy.

The Methodist and the Radical movements came into conflict. The attitude to civil government that was proper to Methodism was defined in the "Minutes of several conversations with the Rev. J. Wesley and the preachers in connection with him," published in 1779. "None of us shall speak lightly or irreverently of the Government under which we live. The oracles of God command us to be subject to the higher powers, and that Honour the King is thus connected with the fear of God." Preachers who were melting great audiences of rough miners to tears with descriptions of the tenderness or the solemnity of a religion which they heard for the first time, found no difficulty in observing the command. One thing and one thing only was in the mind of preacher and congregation. But when the Methodist Church became a great organisation in the midst of a population like that of Manchester or Leeds, in a world where the justice or injustice of institutions was fiercely debated, the situation became more complicated. The Methodist rule against speaking lightly or irreverently of the Government came to be interpreted as not merely a negative, but a positive duty. On the accession of George the Fourth the Conference presented an address of congratulation speaking of "our undeviating attachment to your illustrious house, your sacred person, and to the unrivalled constitution of our country," an address which provoked a remonstrance from "a well-wisher to Methodism," who said the poor had become from necessity politicians. . . . The Annual Report of the Conference took as conservative a view of popular agitation as any clerical justices. The only references to Trade Unions are severe, and the Chartist movement is condemned in the strongest language. The Wesleyan preachers in the Bath district resolved in 1839 that any Methodist who joined himself to the Chartists should be excluded their body. The Conference of the Methodist New Connexion condemned the strikes of 1843, speaking of the " political demagogues, by whom the masses were misguided and inflamed, and rejoicing that no members of the Connexion were among the leaders of or participators in the disurbance."

Naturally, among so numerous a body as the Methodists, it would be possible to find individual exceptions to what has been said. Things would scarce have improved, and human nature would be but a poor thing if individuals did here and there rise above their creeds and show themselves superior to sectarian injunctions. But that what has been said truly reflects the general trend of the Methodist movement and other Christian movements of the time, there can be no doubt. The truth is, there was no social aim whatever involved in the evangelistic movement. The coarser " sins "—drunkenness, lechery, etc.—were reprobated as they always had been, but there the interest stopped. There was no idea of a purely social change, still less of political reforms. Methodism, said Carlyle, had " its eye forever turned on its own navel, asking itself with torturing anxiety of Hope and Fear, 'Am I right? Am I wrong? Shall I be saved? Shall I not be damned?' What is this at bottom but a new phasis of egoism stretched out into the Infinite: not always the better for its infinitude."

At a later date there was, as might be expected, less open hostility between the claims of labour and the teachings of the Christian sects. Religious leaders can never be altogether uninfluenced by the spirit of the age, and rapid secularisation of life that has gone on during the past hundred years has reacted upon both the teachings of religion and the claims of the Churches. So it happens that labour claims that not so long ago had to fight the organised forces of Christianity are now put forward in the name of Christian teaching. Here and there it is, of course, possible to find the names of a few men whose humanitarian feelings proved stronger than their religious associations, and who claimed better treatment for the poor. But in the main the Labour movement in this country, as in every other country, has grown up, not merely outside the range of organised Christianity, but generally in the teeth of the bitterest opposition to it. The facts speak for themselves.

I am not here concerned with the later stages of the relations between Christianity and Labour. That the modern Labour movement has grown up apart from Christianity—but necessarily not apart from Christians, of a kind—is plain. But in Britain, and more particularly on the Continent, its antagonism to Christianity has been marked. The coquetting of Christianity with Labour within the last generation or two is only what one would expect. But it is clear from the preceding pages that the one constant social function of Christianity has been to encourage loyalty to existing institutions, no matter what their character, so long as they were not unfriendly to the Churches. What Lecky said of the Church of England, that it was "at once the most servile and the most efficient agent of tyranny," applies—certainly as regards efficiency—to all sections of the Christian Church. From Constantine the Great onward, the world's rulers have patronised it and upheld it for its own ends, and the character of its friends condemns it with more deadly certainty than the attacks of its enemies.

In the foregoing pages we have seen how little truth there is in the statement that Christianity destroyed chattel-slavery. We have also seen the falsity of the claim that it minimised or abolished social wrong by spreading abroad a spirit of humanity and brotherhood. Neither of these claims can withstand careful examination. Slavery and the oppression of labour continued while Christianity was at its strongest and wealthiest—its own wealth being derived from the oppression it encouraged. Slavery died out when social and economic conditions rendered its continuance more and more difficult. And the conditions of labour improved when men ceased to talk of a "Providential order," of "God's decree," dismissed the evangelical narcotic served out by the Churches, and began to realise that social conditions were the products of understandable and modifiable natural forces.

VII.

Black and White

◆ ◆

To have dealt earlier with the relation of the Black and White peoples and the treatment of the former by the latter, would have diverted attention from the main point at issue. So many other questions intrude themselves here that in discussing the non-essential points (non-essential, that is, to the question of Christianity and Slavery), the essential one might have been missed. Nevertheless, a glance at the subject cannot but be enlightening, particularly when one bears in mind the fact that the conquering white professes the Christian religion, and that in nearly every case his conquest is advanced under cover of giving to the coloured peoples a purer religion and a higher civilisation.

Stripped of all pretence and subterfuge, the history of the relations of the white to the black races, as of the " lower " races generally, is a record of subjugation and exploitation, and of subjugation for the purpose of exploitation. Both the subjugation and exploitation may be more or less paternal and kindly, or it may be exploitation naked and unashamed; but it is always there. The white man is among the coloured peoples to further his own interests, and where an alert, instructed, and enlightened public opinion does not hold him in check, these interests are promoted with but scant regard for the subject peoples concerned.[97a] Everywhere we have the same story of the obtaining of " concessions " from native chiefs under misleading pretexts, of childish bribes, or deliberate fraud. And once the land is acquired the next step is to discover by what means the natives may be forced to " steady and continuous work if the local conditions are such that *from the mere bounty of nature all the ambitions of the people can be gratified without any considerable amount of labour.*"[98] The earlier method of securing labour was by slavery. That, however, was crude, and the term is distasteful. So with the assistance of the Indenture system in India, the sending out of native police in S. Africa (prior to 1897) to " collect " labour, or the Glen Grey Act, or the compound system, or the location system, or an ingeniously devised hut tax, we do manage to get the labour per-

[97a] I have no space to enter into details here, but the reader who consults such works as *Blacks and Whites in South Africa*, by Fox Bourne or Professor Gilbert Murray's essay on " The Exploitation of the Lower Races " in *Liberalism and the Empire*, will be able to judge the value of the professions of benevolence served out to a public easily, perhaps willingly, befooled.

[98] Professor Ireland, *Tropical Colonization*, p. 155.

formed "essential for the proper development of the country," to cite Cecil Rhodes.[99] And where the race cannot be brought to appreciate the benefits of labouring to develop a country for the benefit of the white, the disappearing or disappeared Tasmanians, Bushmen, Red Indians, etc., give another end to the story. However much to the benefit of white "civilisation" the subjection of the coloured peoples may have been, there is little doubt that it has brought few real benefits to these "lower" peoples. Generally speaking, we have succeeded in breaking down most of their native virtues, and presented them in return with a good share of our own vices.

The clearest case of recent years of the exploita-

[99] I have already given some specimens of the advertisements in English and American papers during the time that slavery was a recognized institution. One may place at the side of these the following from a Natal newspaper only a few years back: "Absconded, an indentured Indian named 'Munsuamy'; discolouration of skin on left side of chest and left cheek. Also indentured Indian named 'Ponusamy'; scar on right shoulder blade, mole on right palm. —Anyone harbouring same will be prosecuted." (Cited by J. G. Godard, *Racial Supremacy*, p. 252.) It must be remembered that this advertisement does not refer to negroes, but to natives of our Indian Empire, who have been brought to Africa under the Indenture system, and against which protests are constantly made by educated Hindoos. Some idea of the conditions prevailing with these indentured labourers may be gathered from a statement made by the Colonial Secretary in the House of Commons on June 30, 1904. He then stated that while the number of suicides among the "free" Indians was 156 per million, among indentured Indians it was 766.

tion of coloured peoples by whites is that furnished by the history of the Congo Free State under the control of the pious Leopold, King of Belgium.[100]

Before 1874 the Congo basin was a well-populated district, inhabited by a number of uncivilised tribes. These tribes were engaged more or less in tribal wars, which were largely a result of contact with the whites, since they were generated and perpetuated chiefly on account of slave raids. It was also at this period that there developed an intensified " scramble for Africa." England, France and Portugal already owned possessions there, and Germany and Italy became also desirous of acquiring possessions. So also did Belgium, which had been an independent kingdom under Leopold since 1831. Leopold's method was to form an International African Association—of course, with the usual professions of piety and disinterestedness. A lavish expenditure on the Press and in other directions gained for the Association the support of public opinion in Britain; and largely in order to check the supposed designs of France, Great Britain agreed to a West African Conference in 1884. The Conference opened its sittings " in the name of Almighty God," and the result of its deliberations was the handing over of certain territory to the control of the International African

[100] My main authorities for the case of the Congo are *Red Rubber,* by E. D. Morel; *King Leopold's Soliloquy,* by Mark Twain; and *The Congo and the Coasts of Africa,* by Richard Harding Davis.

Association, under certain stipulated conditions. Needless to say, no representative of the natives was present at the Conference. The Conference gave what didn't belong to it to an Association that had no claim to what it received. In August, 1885, King Leopold notified the signatories that his Association would henceforth be known as the "Congo Free State," and that he himself was monarch of the domain.

The whole of the population of the area was thus handed over, and the cruelty and heartless exploitation of the people almost passes belief. A population of about two millions was converted by a stroke of the pen into a nation of slaves, under the control of officials whose brutalities beggar description. The Belgian Secretary of State wrote to the Governor-General that the officials "must neglect no means of exploiting the forests," and they did not. They were paid a bonus on the rubber and ivory collected, and at the point of the rifle and to the crack of the whip the natives were driven forth to collect what was required. Villages were raided, the natives seized, and released in order to collect the ivory and rubber. Nearly fourteen million pounds' worth of goods was forced from the natives in seven years. If the people refused or rebelled, or failed to bring in what was required, punishment—death or mutilation, or death and mutilation—followed. Some few travellers and missionaries sent home to England and America reports of the atrocities

—reports that were discreetly shelved. The native troops employed proved their zeal in bringing back to their officers *the severed hands* of those who had been murdered—in one case 160 hands, in other cases fifty or eighty. This, said our own Consul, was not the native custom; it was "the deliberate act of the soldiers of a European administration . . . obeying the positive orders of their superiors." The photographs published in Mark Twain's book of the children so treated place the fact of the mutilations beyond doubt.

Whole districts were depopulated. Of eight villages with a population of over 3,000, only ten persons were left. Of another district the population dropped in fifteen years from 50,000 to 5,000. The Bolangi tribe, formerly numbering 40,000, sank to 8,000. King Leopold, it is calculated, netted a profit of between three and five millions sterling, and could call God to witness the purity of his motives and his desire to promote civilisation.

So long as possible, both Governments and missionary societies burked investigation of the atrocities reported. The matter was first raised in our own Parliament by Sir Charles Dilke in 1897. Some sort of an official report was prepared, but no further Parliamentary notice worth recording was taken until 1903. The "official" reports were suppressed—lock, stock and barrel." The British Government contented itself with "private representations to Leopold."

The silence of the missionary societies was equally striking. Mr. Morel points out that, although plenty of information was available, the executives of the missionary societies took no action, and, " with three exceptions," no missionary gave public expression to his experiences until October, 1903. The Roman Catholic missionaries were altogether silent until 1903 —was not Leopold a devout Catholic? And when Mr. Morel visited the United States of America in 1904 to ventilate the Congo horror, he was bitterly opposed by Cardinal Gibbon, the leading Catholic ecclesiastic in the United States.

This is the most recent story, although one of the most horrible, of the action of the Christian whites in relation to the " uncivilised " blacks. Does " heathen " records furnish anything that would eclipse it in sheer horror? What restraining or humanising influence had Christianity here? May it not even be that Christianity had an influence in dulling the perception of many to this century's long exploitation of the " lower " races? It has already been pointed out that the development of the " colour bar " is largely a product of the Christian centuries. Between the " saved " and the " lost," Christianity drew a deep and fundamental distinction, and it may well be that this, together with the outlet for moral energy in the work of evangelisation as an anodyne for scoundrels, and in other forms of religious enterprise,

Christianity has made this game of pious exploitation the easier.

Into that question I have no present intention of entering. It is enough to have shown how systematic and continuous has been the perpetuation of various forms of wrong under Christian auspices. And if, in spite of all, the world does move in the direction of larger views and a more humanitarian ethic, we have to look for the causes in the normal development of social life under the impulses of justice and common sense.